POWER WOMEN WORLDWIDE

CALLED TO LEAD

SUCCESS STRATEGIES FOR WOMEN

PEGINE ECHEVARRIA
MSW, HoF, CVP

+ 17 INSPIRATIONAL WOMEN

Called to Lead

First published in 2021 by

Panoma Press Ltd
48 St Vincent Drive, St Albans, Herts, AL1 5SJ, UK
info@panomapress.com
www.panomapress.com

Book layout by Neil Coe.

978-1-784529-36-9

The rights of Ulrike Aichhorn, Barbara Baron, Patricia Baxter, Julie Cottineau, Jessica Devenish, Dianne Devitt, Pegine Echevarria, Jennifer Einolf, Mindy Gibbins-Klein, Donna Hanson, Sydne Jacques, Carla Johnston, Shanna Kabatznick, Cindy Tschosik, Diana Watson, Jill Whipple, Bonnie Wims and Catherine Woodhouse to be identified as the authors of this work have been asserted in accordance with sections 77 and 78 of the Copyright, Designs and Patents Act 1988.

A CIP catalogue record for this book is available from the British Library.

This book is available online and in bookstores.

DEDICATION

Dedicated to women worldwide who are called to lead.

Thank you for heeding the call.

*To an incredible Leader —
ABBONDANZA !!!*

*May you always make time
for a meal with family & friends!*

Barbara

Chapter 17

TESTIMONIALS

As a transitioning veteran and a woman with experience leading in junior and middle management in male-dominated industries, I'm constantly seeking advice from experienced women leaders. Having *Called to Lead* as a resource has been invaluable for me. The Action Steps in this book make it stand miles apart from other resources because they provide applicable, actionable, realistic, and inspiring advice for me to improve in every dimension of my leadership. This wisdom in this book empowers me with the strength to stand out, and the knowledge to help me do so in a way that empowers my team, enhances my organization, and paves the way for new, innovative, forward-thinking leaders behind me.

Danielle V., MIT Sloan MBA,
U.S. Military Officer, Corporate Leader

Reading the insights of 18 leaders sharing their expertise and wisdom about how they lead, tips for the reader and real usable advice from the trenches was educational. Looking forward to sharing this book with our talent development program and women's leadership program.

Jessica George,
Vice President Relationship Manager

This book gave me insights and wisdom to grow as a leader. My natural leadership received a boost after reading this book. Now I want my senior leaders to read it, they can use the advice too!

**L.P.M, 30-year-old,
Human Resource Benefits Leader**

Called to Lead is for women who are leaders as well as women who want to be leaders. *Called to Lead* is a roadmap for success told in diverse stories and voices. The women in this book share their path to leadership, their words to live by as well as the path you can follow to step into your own powerful leader mode.

**Sandy Weaver, Program Director,
Center for Workplace Happiness**

ACKNOWLEDGEMENTS

This book would not be possible without the diligence, support, and hours of editing, reviewing, and thoughtful, detailed work by Lindsay Murtagh.

Professional ghostwriter, leader, and gifted intuitive Cindy Tschosik gave selflessly to this project as a guest editor. She worked with authors to craft their chapters so that you, the reader, have an immersive experience.

Mindy Gibbins-Klein called me early one morning with a dream; she didn't know that I had the same vision that night. We laughed, conspired, and discussed this collaboration and our community of women leaders worldwide. How can we get them to share their brilliance with other women called to lead? This book is the result of that dream – the first book of Power Women Worldwide.

I am eternally grateful for my Mom, who passed this year. She was a leader, a businesswoman, a powerhouse, a teacher, and my mentor. Her energy, enthusiasm, and passion for women, who are called to lead, flow throughout this book.

For our moms. Many of us have lost our moms. No matter the relationship we had with our mothers, it is clear that they had an influence and an impact. They inspired us to be who we have become. Thank you for raising such amazing women, the authors in this book.

Thank you to my husband, business partner, soulmate, and supporter of women everywhere. David Herbin, you indeed are a special man. To my son, Kenneth, thank you for your service, you are a great man. Thank you to my daughter, Andrea, for your guidance, wisdom, and editing for my chapter and the book; you are indeed a powerful woman.

I am deeply grateful for the passion of these 17 brilliant authors. They continually serve, support, and mentor women leaders worldwide. In the chapters ahead, they share their truth, advice and action steps − always with you, a woman called to lead, in mind.

POWER WOMEN WORLDWIDE LEADERS, YOUR AUTHORS

1. Pegine Echevarria, MSW, HoF, CVP
    UNITED STATES

2. Jill Whipple
    UNITED STATES

3. Mindy Gibbins-Klein, MBA, CVP
    UNITED KINGDOM

4. Julie Cottineau
    UNITED STATES

5. Dianne Devitt
    UNITED STATES

6. Jennifer Einolf, PCC, NCC, DTM
    UNITED STATES

7. Dr. Carla Johnston
    UNITED STATES

8. Shanna Kabatznick
    ECUADOR/UNITED STATES

9. Ulrike Aichhorn, MAS, MTD, CSP
    AUSTRIA

10. Diana Watson, MA, MS, DTM
    TAIWAN

11. Catherine Woodhouse, MD
    UNITED STATES

12. Dr. Bonnie Wims
    UNITED STATES

13. Cindy Tschosik
    UNITED STATES

14. Dr. Patricia (Pat) Baxter
    UNITED STATES

15. Donna Hanson, CSP
    AUSTRALIA

16. Jessica Devenish
    UNITED STATES

17. Barbara Baron, MS, RDN, CDN, FAND
    UNITED STATES

18. Sydne Jacques, PE, CSP
    UNITED STATES

PREFACE

Women who are called to lead are a unique breed of women. They usually are noticed first by others. It is our dream that eventually they embrace their leadership moxie. We know you, we are you, and we want to support you so you thrive. Statistics show women are moving up rank as leaders and that over 10% of all working-age women are entrepreneurs. These women are leading businesses now and in the future. We are progressing and as women heed the call to lead, we grow in numbers.

Power Women Worldwide is for women in leadership and those in business. We provide training, development, and support for you to shine, to grow, to expand, and to honor your gift of leadership. Leadership is both an inherent calling and mixture of development, skill enhancement, and mind shift. Our conferences, training, membership groups, and masterminds are for women called to lead. We specialize in Power Women, women leaders who are unique and called to lead. Our goal is for them to embrace their internal power and lead positively worldwide.

Called to Lead addresses your call to leadership, giving you the developmental skills you need to thrive and the mind shift you must have to succeed as a leader. Our goal is for you to invest in your natural leadership calling so that you can manage more complex issues, have a more abundant, exhilarating life, and still be at peace, refreshed, and confident in your calling.

Called to Lead has five segments, with several chapters in each segment:

- ✦ The Power of Being Called to Lead

- ✦ The Power of Self-Mastery in Leadership

- ✦ The Power of Influential Leadership

- ✦ The Power of Emotions and The Mind in Leadership

- ✦ The Power of Leadership Love

Each chapter has:

Her Passion and Story ✦ Each author has a different leadership journey and passion. Diversity is key to learning and each leader's story is unique. Knowing a person's power enables you to grow your own power.

Her Quote ✦ A quote the author created for herself. She lives by her quote; it has meaning to her leadership and life.

Advice for Her ✦ As your advisor, she shares her advice for your journey as a leader.

Action Steps for Her ✦ Steps you can take in the next 24 hours to one week that can make a difference in your life and leadership.

CONTENTS

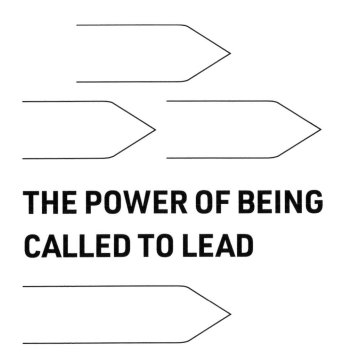

THE POWER OF BEING
CALLED TO LEAD

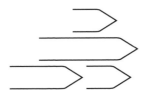

CHAPTER 1

CALLED TO LEAD – INFLUENCE, IMPACT, AND INSPIRE OTHERS

PEGINE ECHEVARRIA, MSW, HoF, CVP

Do you find yourself experiencing an innate force driving you to influence others?

If so, you are CALLED TO LEAD. I am, too. Since my teen years, I've always been tapped to lead a project, organize an event, or oversee a project. I couldn't recognize what supervisors saw in me. I was young when I realized that I was able to lead others; I knew I was different.

My name is Pegine. I have spoken to audiences worldwide on leadership, and I am an award-winning businesswoman who appears in leading news outlets. I have organized a significant event for a President of the United States, produced leadership experiences for thousands of military officers, and I lead Power Women Worldwide, an organization that empowers women to be bold, be brave, be seen, be heard, and be paid well. I know what it feels like and means to be CALLED TO LEAD.

By reading this book, you already know or at least have a feeling that you are also called. It's time to accept that you're CALLED TO LEAD. Your desire to influence, impact and inspire others to action is who you are in your heart and soul. When you are called to lead, you tap into a gift; it's your power. What you do is "normal" to you. You are unique. Not everyone is called, and oftentimes, we discount our gifts or talents that come naturally. We assume that everyone has such a blessing.

At a certain point, you realize you are "supposed" to lead. It's your role. You may have uncomfortable feelings. Yes, you are different from most people. You come to recognize your calling is a responsibility. It became my responsibility to nurture my gift, and I had to embrace that gift and use it for positive, powerful outcomes. You are CALLED TO LEAD. Now it's time for you to own your power to influence, impact and inspire others.

When we finally accept that we are called to lead and we are different, it opens all possibilities. Embracing that responsibility sets you on a journey of self-discovery.

You want to:

+ Understand how you do what you do, beyond instinct

+ Examine your thought process

+ Challenge yourself to think bigger, bolder, and more positively about yourself and your future as a leader

+ Improve your strategy

As a young girl and teen, I always organized events, and took charge of school projects and school plays. During college and graduate school, I led coalitions and collaboratives. I took my leadership skills for granted. When I opened the business in Spain, I didn't think what I was doing was out of the ordinary. When I was a working mother of young children, I led my sales division, held board positions, and volunteered in my children's school. I realized this wasn't "normal." Not everyone took opportunities to lead inside and outside of work. I desired to make better communities and better organizations. I struggled with the strong need for me to step in. I couldn't understand why I felt the desire to speak up and be in charge. It was later when I saw them as my gifts. I learned to invest in myself, improve and embrace myself as a leader. That's why I'm so excited to be sharing the lessons that I've learned with you today.

I was CALLED TO LEAD. I had no idea that my career or life would be what it has become. Being able to follow the calling and investing in my growth is a game-changer. Isn't that the same for you? You, too, are CALLED TO LEAD with influence, impact, and the ability to inspire others.

During our leadership development, we often become loners. We push people away, not allowing people to help us. However, for us to move to higher leadership levels and take on bigger tasks, more significant missions, and have a bigger purpose, we must learn how to delegate well, influence people to act on our behalf, and build positive relationships.

Three Keys to Master Your Leadership

Key 1: Influence and Persuasion. Influence is crucial to leading others. It's the capacity to cause a change in someone or something. You have influence. Learn persuasion skills, psychology, sales techniques, the diversity of people's thought processes, and how to leverage your innate abilities. Why are you charismatic? Your influence is key to leadership development.

Key 2: Impact. Successful leadership calls for your impact to strongly affect someone or something. Your impact isn't subtle and has the power to effect change. How does your strength of character affect people so they trust you? Providing results for others is an important personal development skill, too. To achieve impact, discover and embrace who you are, strengthen your faith and believe in your abilities. Know your moral compass and know these values are *your* choices. You get to decide: Who do I want to be? How do I want to lead? This decision requires self-inquiry, reflection, and education. Incorporate journaling, meditation, take workshops, and increase self-knowledge to gain self-confidence, self-love, and awareness of your abilities and power. Invest in yourself; it's critical to becoming a powerful communicator, a more confident woman, and a strong leader.

Key 3: Inspiration. Inspiration is the process of being mentally stimulated to do or feel something. Your words matter. Your presence matters. How you speak to people, communicate to them, and draw them in matters. Your ability to stimulate them and feel your passion matters. People selected you to be their leader. Leadership is not a title given by your job; it is an honor bestowed on you by those who follow you.

To have influence, impact, and inspire others requires continuous self-development work.

Her Quote

"Be Bold, Be Brave, Be Seen, Be Heard and Be Paid Well." – Pegine

Advice for Her

Be Bold. Boldness requires courage and conviction. As a woman compelled to lead, raise your hand, share your opinion, and seek solutions for big problems. Be bold, build relationships before your meetings, and before sharing your ideas in front of a group. Seek others who will support your opinions and your vision. Building those relationships requires boldness. Let people know who you are. Ask for an informational meeting. Share your and your team's successes to an influencer or leader who can and will talk positively about you in their discussions with others. Boldly seek advocates.

Be Brave. Bravery is the hallmark of leadership. Courage is easier to express when you put others at the forefront of your mission. Knowing you will speak up to help others is one of the hallmarks of women in leadership. Being a champion for others is brave. Be brave for your department, your division, and your organization. Believe in what you do. Have faith in yourself and your ability to deliver results. People love following a brave leader. Inspire them with your bravery.

Be Seen. Leaders must be seen. Speaking before groups, being on panels, and sharing your wisdom are powerful ways to influence, impact, and inspire others – volunteer for these experiences. Top leaders invest in their skills as presenters and influencers. Market yourself in subtle ways to gain roles that can change their organization and the world. No matter the level you are in "officially" as a leader, take responsibility, and be seen.

Be Heard. Your ideas, solutions, insights, and wisdom are valuable. Waiting for the perfect time to share your knowledge is not in your highest, best good. There is no ideal time. If you discover a solution, speak up. Women often think, "what will they think of me?" Sadly, they say that statement with trepidation. They rarely think, "*they are going to love me!*" You must invest in your confidence, thoughts, and skills. Be heard to lead well.

Be Paid Well. Your leadership gifts are valuable to all organizations. In my work with women leaders, I encounter them undervaluing their worth. Often, women don't negotiate; they accept what is offered, which leaves money, opportunities, and benefits on the table. Knowing your worth and asking for your worth is a critical leadership skill. Develop a prosperity mindset and learn to negotiate.

Action Steps for Her

1. **Own the room.** If you're leading a meeting or about to present, get there early. Walk around the room; imagine where you'll be sitting. Stretch out your arms and say, "I own this room."

2. **Build your confidence.** Each level of leadership requires another level of confidence. Learn how to embrace the four pillars of leadership confidence. You can enroll in my Confidence Karma online course at www.confidencekarma.online

3. **Ask questions.** Master curiosity. Seek answers. Questions open doors.

4. **Smile.** The power of the smile opens doors, disarms people, and creates community.

You *are* a leader. Embrace your gift. Invest in yourself and your leadership skills. The world wants and needs women who lead. **Be Bold. Be Brave. Be Seen. Be Heard. Be Paid Well. Be You**.

PEGINE ECHEVARRIA

MSW, HoF, CVP
UNITED STATES

Quoted in *The New York Times, Forbes, The Wall Street Journal* and featured on *Speaker* and *Minority Business Enterprise* magazines. Pegine, who goes by her first name, is the only Latina in the Motivational Speakers Hall of Fame, alongside stars like Jack Canfield. Through Power Women Worldwide groups, she focuses on uplifting women in leadership, making her one of the Society for Human Resource Management's 100 Global Thought Leaders on Diversity & Inclusion. Her experience and influence encompasses business and entrepreneurship – as the founder and leader of multi-million-dollar businesses; education – as a speaker, presenter, therapist, and mentor. Pegine has received business recognition from organizations including the Women's Business Minority National Council, U.S. Department of Defense, and U.S. Small Business Administration, which named her a Women in Business Champion.

Learn more

Website: www.powerwomenworldwide.com

Linkedin: www.linkedin.com/in/pegine

Facebook: www.facebook.com/powerwomenworldwide

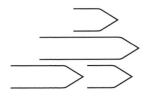

CHAPTER 2

CALLED TO LEAD - REMOTE LEADING

JILL WHIPPLE

As the pandemic of 2020 unfolded, and corporations pivoted to remote work, I realized that my leading remote teams for over 20 years was a skill I took for granted. As a technology leader working for a large financial company, with sites in many locations including global partners, it was normal for me to engage with team members, peers and leadership who were not physically located where I was. I was called to lead remotely, this is a skill. I polished this skill through trial and error over many years, learning that trusting my gut leadership instincts was critical. I knew when someone was ready to be challenged further, when someone was struggling and needed guidance, or when someone was not meeting expectations. Not unlike leaders with teams sitting within the same four walls, the difference is you are leading and communicating over the phone or technology versus face to face.

Her Quote

"It's not where you lead from, it's how you lead."
– Jill Whipple

We are all called to lead, whether as a leader of a small team, large organization, or an individual contributor; you are still leading and influencing. You do not need to be physically co-located to do so. It is important to recognize this, embrace who you are and your leadership style. You will need to tweak some aspects of how you lead virtually, such as increasing communication and different ways of communicating. A dear friend of mine has been a successful professional coach for many years, she has global recognition, and the majority of her coaching is via phone. She has proven you can be successful without being in the same room. I have been just as successful and so can you.

Advice for Her

Trust your instincts and constantly communicate in many different ways. One of the biggest obstacles in leading remotely is not being able to easily read a person's body language. Trust your instincts on what you are picking up from your discussions. Ask open-ended questions and then pause and embrace the silence for them to answer. Keep probing and encourage them to talk. I learned this the hard way. I thought I had a great and open relationship with someone on my team and everything was fine. I knew she had been going through some tough personal times, but I was confident I was right there with her. Several months after a team building meeting, she opened up that she disrespected someone I invited to present at the meeting. This was an "aha moment" for me and truly impacted my leadership style. I was not probing enough, asking questions, or fully listening. Doing so remotely is a critical skill to build, and I changed based on this experience to ask more open-ended questions after meetings to gather insight. The result has been at times a bit uncomfortable in hearing the feedback, but in the long run critical to my team's overall growth and delivering business results.

Action Steps for Her

Here are my Top Ten action steps for successfully leading a remote team. Many are not different from leading in a brick-and-mortar office, they just have nuances:

1. **Bookending the day.** Engaging your team at the beginning and end of the day, which I call Bookending, is essential. I schedule a 15-minute virtual "stand-up" in the morning. The focus is for each team member to share what was accomplished the previous day, what is today's goal, and are they encountering any roadblocks. If there are any roadblocks, I or other team members can help address them afterward. At the end of the day, I reach out individually to each person to see how their day went and if they need anything from

me. This approach results in an engaged team, built on trust.

2. **Choice of meetings.** New technology enabling video meetings is a great tool. However, people do not always want to be seen, especially close up and if they are not having a great day. Ask your team their preference for meetings – phone or video. This also instills that you respect them. Another option is to offer every other meeting as video and then phone. This will provide them the opportunity to be "on" versus "not so on" and make the meetings more engaging, which is ultimately what you want to achieve.

3. **Ongoing communication.** Communication is a critical skill for every successful leader, even more so when leading a remote team. It is easy for team members to feel isolated when not sitting with their team. Implementing multiple ways to communicate with your team and others on the team is critical. Some tried and true ways to disseminate information are a monthly formal written communication to the team, or periodic full team meetings. Focus groups with a smaller number of team members are a great way to gain insight from your team, by asking a few open-ended questions for discussion. Lastly, one-on-one meetings enable you to review their achievements, impediments and provide ongoing coaching.

4. **Trust they are working.** One of the biggest concerns leaders have is they cannot physically see their team members and know they are working.

It is imperative you build trust with your team and recognize they will not be at their computer the entire eight hours. It is OK if they step away for a break, to grab a cup of coffee, or even change out the laundry. Rather than focus on if they are working, shift the focus on the business value they are providing. Define realistic objectives and metrics to measure. Review the status and outcomes at one-on-one meetings. Positive results always speak for themselves, as do missed deliverables and excuses.

5. **Showcase your team.** This one is especially important, as your leadership does not naturally interact with your team in a remote environment, as they might in a brick-and-mortar one. You need to strategically invite them to meetings to present and participate, not just listen. The goal is to showcase their brilliance, enabling your leadership to engage with them, gain their insight, and learn about the results they are contributing to the business. This will increase your team member's confidence in their competence, while enhancing their career growth.

6. **Engage the quiet.** We have all been in meetings where someone (or several people) never spoke a word. These are typically those more introverted, or quiet, yet in a one-on-one discussion they provide great insight. A remote working environment can increase their reluctance to engage. As a leader, you should ask for their input and opinions during the meeting. Even better, prior to the meeting, discuss with them your

plan and help them strategize their response. They will be prepared and confident to express their opinions.

7. **Executive "presence."** Many think of this as how you show up in appearance and present yourself in meetings. That is part of it but more importantly is being present as a leader and available when your team needs you. It is the open-door policy. Create virtual office hours where team members can pop in for a chat. Keep your instant messaging open with your team and encourage engagement for quick questions. Let them know the times you are unavailable. This is another way to build trust and respect.

8. **Continually assess.** Constant and ongoing change has become a norm. This is no different if you are brick-and-mortar or remote. It is imperative you continually assess your team, how they are doing and how the team is doing in delivering business value. Take the time periodically to get input from your team, either via meetings and discussions or surveys. Once you get their input, reflect on the information, and identify potential changes to implement. Further engage your team to discuss and refine the changes, along with implementation action steps. This also ensures you have their commitment, resulting in successful improvements.

9. **Celebrate!** Celebrating team successes and milestones virtually requires some creativity. This can be as simple as holding up a handmade "Thank You" sign during a video meeting, holding a virtual happy

hour, or sending treat boxes for snacking during a virtual meeting. Whether you are celebrating a small or large success, it does not matter how, it matters that you take the time to do so. Your team will stay engaged.

10. **Do not forget about you.** I love leading people, watching them develop, grow, and succeed. It can be easy to forget about nourishing yourself as a leader. Take time for your own continued growth. Block time on your calendar for strategic thinking and to complete critical work deliverables. Ensure you have a mentor, engage in development programs, and take time to reflect on your career development. Read a book, watch a podcast, work out, join a professional organization – there are so many ways to enrich yourself. Doing so will make you a better leader.

JILL WHIPPLE

UNITED STATES

Jill Whipple recently retired from a large financial company after a stellar 30-plus year career. Jill is a technology leader with expertise in program management that delivers strong business results. She has also led governance programs delivering risk identification, mitigation, and control services to the organization. Throughout her career, she honed her ability to lead remote teams successfully, while consistently delivering business value.

Jill is a highly motivational leader with a participative style who builds strong relationships and can adapt to lead in different environments. Jill has a passion for talent development, mentoring employees and is a mentor for Women Unlimited LEAD, Orlando.

Jill has a Bachelor of Science in Computer Science from Stetson University. She resides in Jacksonville, Florida with her husband Paul and two children.

Learn more

LinkedIn: www.linkedin.com/in/jill-whipple

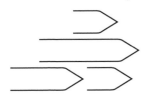

CHAPTER 3

CALLED TO LEAD – INCLUSIVE THOUGHTFUL LEADERSHIP

MINDY GIBBINS-KLEIN, MBA, CVP

WHY do I feel called to lead in this area? Several reasons, in fact. Firstly, truly thoughtful leadership is sorely lacking in many areas. We hear a lot about thought leadership, but most of what is labelled thought leadership is not original. It's often missing the kind of thought that would make it truly exceptional. As a result, it just adds to the noise.

Secondly, the areas of leadership and thought leadership still tend to be dominated by middle-aged white men. I don't have a problem with middle-aged white men, in fact I'm married to one! But we need more diverse content in leadership books, conferences, and other media. People from under-represented groups don't see enough people like them being published and showcased, therefore they don't believe they will be seen or heard, so they don't tend to step up and so a vicious cycle is allowed to continue.

I must admit that when I see a list of recommended business books without even one female author or person of color listed, I have a visceral reaction. I feel sad but also quite angry and frustrated. That's how I know there's more work to be done and I am the one who has been called to do it. So, I gather all my resources together and keep pushing forward.

This is not just tokenism. I believe with all my heart and soul that we need diverse voices and points of view to take our society to the next level of its evolution. We need our bookshelves, events, social media feeds and important conversations to reflect the society we live in. When one dominant group is the main group that is visible and vocal, we miss out on new ideas that could spark further new ideas and progress. Despite good intentions, the dominant group creates a kind of group-think or echo chamber, with the same ideas circulating around, albeit occasionally with a new spin or angle.

Diversity is a possibility. Inclusion is a goal. Inclusivity is the honest admission that the playing field is not level, plus the work to level it. Equity goes one step further, giving extra help and support to those who need it more than others so they can be included. I do the work I do because my personal mission is to create equity for all people from under-represented groups and those who feel that left to chance, they are not being given a fair chance.

Her Quote

"The world needs you to have your best thoughts
and your biggest thoughts."
– Mindy GK (first published in *The Thoughtful Leader*
(Panoma Press 2015)

You know what it feels like when you have a really good thought or idea. Your heart swells with pride and beats that little bit faster in anticipation of what you could create. Then something happens. Doubt creeps in. You think of all the obstacles that stand in your way, and all the work involved in getting this idea going or into the market. After all, it is a big idea. And who are you to think you can run with this and make it happen? So many times, it is relegated to the back burner.

Another terrible outcome is when you have the idea and even start the planning, but fears stop you from sharing it or taking it to completion. Women tend to fear rejection more than their male counterparts, and it can seem easier to drop it than to be shot down. Women also don't tend to like coming across as egotistical, and so much of what is called thought leadership is about ego. So, it is not surprising that women think themselves out of some of their best ideas!

Here's the great news: we do think more. Therefore, all we need to do is channel that thinking into ways to get our ideas out there, instead of squashing them. Thoughtful leadership involves putting more thought and consideration into the people you engage with, and the ideas you share with them. It puts the customer at the heart (literally) of the message. Perfect for those who tend to be thoughtful!

In terms of thinking bigger and playing a bigger role, this simply requires a better strategy. Women and other minorities are certainly capable of ground-breaking, thought-leading ideas and it is refreshing when we hear from new voices. All progress depends on new thinking.

Advice for Her

This may sound like a strange suggestion when you are reading a book, but stop reading. I don't mean right now. Finish reading this chapter and this book, taking notes and planning the actions you wish to take when you finish it. What I'm asking you to consider is the amount of time and effort you put into reading and listening to everyone else's content in your topic or area. Thought leadership does not come from curating others' ideas, and thoughtful leadership is not possible when you are under the influence of everyone else's voices.

An insidious feeling can arise, of not having anything new to say. This actually comes from reading too much and giving too much credit and importance to all the other so-called thought leaders. Stop. Give yourself the time and space to think.

The most important thing you can decide – right now – is what you want to be known for. What message do you want to be known for, as well as your achievements? Just having the clarity around your purpose and message, knowing exactly where you play and how you add value, gives you enormous confidence and allows you to relax.

When you feel confident, you are also much more likely to find yourself in situations where you can help others. If you are in a position of leadership, use your influence for good. Reach a hand out, or down, to help another woman and lift her up. Seek out opportunities to help other people from under-represented groups to get to the table, share their important insights and make a bigger impact.

Action Steps for Her

Commit to being more thoughtful. Now is the time to make things happen, dear thoughtful leader. Now is the time to crystallize your ideas and share them intentionally. If you feel inspired after reading this book, make a decision to become the kind of leader you know deep down you already are. Making a decision is easy to do – it costs nothing and can be done in an instant – but we tend to make it into a big issue in our mind. Just ask your heart if you desire to be a truly thoughtful leader. If so, say yes. By the way, it's fine if your answer is no. Thoughtful leadership is a choice.

Create some space and think about the people and issues where you need to be thoughtful right now. You may be struggling with an interpersonal relationship, which the right consideration and approach could turn around.

You will probably need to schedule the time to do this important work. I call it Thinking and Consideration Time, and that contains both meanings of consideration. Actually put some TCT slots in your calendar if you can, to give you a better chance of success.

Have a process for your thinking. As a leader, you probably rely on different processes for your work and they help you get things done more effectively and efficiently. Thinking is no different; it's just that we don't tend to hear about this or learn this skill at school. I'm happy to have a chat anytime about the processes we use at REAL Thought Leaders, so just ask.

Be firm yet gentle with yourself. This may sound like a contradiction so let me explain. Be firm when it comes to going for your goals and reaching your highest potential. Don't let fear, other people or distractions pull you in the wrong direction. People around you may have their own reasons for questioning, criticizing or even sabotaging you. That is not your concern. Love them and continue to respect them. You may need to pull yourself back to your commitment and vision with a firm hand. You may need to do this several times, many times or constantly. Every time you do, you will move forward with more strength, resolve and determination.

If (when) you get it wrong — the tone, the message, the result — be gentle with yourself and praise yourself for the intention, the effort and the energy you brought to that task. Give yourself a hug, then commit to having another attempt, this time with the knowledge and insights from the previous attempt.

Celebrate every single win. Every time you get it right, acknowledge it and celebrate. You are becoming one of the most thoughtful leaders in your organization, society and possibly even the planet! What a thought! It's so easy to focus on mistakes and perceived failures, ignoring successes, when in fact all the little wins add up to your success.

MINDY GIBBINS-KLEIN

MBA, CVP
UNITED KINGDOM

Mindy Gibbins-Klein is a multi-award-winning international speaker, thought leadership strategist, book coach and publisher. She has authored and co-authored 10 books, and has presented to and coached over 50,000 business executives and entrepreneurs in 18 countries. Mindy created The Book Midwife® brand, and designed the methodology that has helped over one thousand leaders to take their ideas and turn them into thought-leading books.

Her content has been syndicated, licensed, and showcased worldwide and her TEDx talk "Sometimes You Need to Change Yourself to Be Yourself" has had nearly one million views and showcases Mindy's insights on living life more thoughtfully.

A native New Yorker, Mindy currently lives near London with her long-suffering husband who tries everything he can think of to get her to take time off.

Learn more

Website: www.mindygk.com

Website: www.bookmidwife.com

All other platforms and links: http://linktr.ee/mindygk

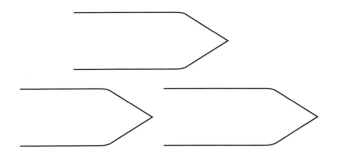

THE POWER OF SELF-MASTERY IN LEADERSHIP

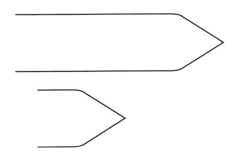

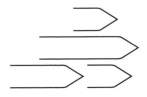

CHAPTER 4

CALLED TO LEAD – BRAND OF YOU

JULIE COTTINEAU

You are a brand!

It's your personal brand that adds credibility to your profile as a leader and helps you stand out among a sea of other credentialed professionals. Brands are stories and your personal brand is the story of you, how you want to be seen, and your special qualities. When we think of our favorite story lines in movies, books, TV shows, often they have a twist – something unique and unexpected that sets them apart and sticks in our minds long after we've finished reading or watching. It's the same thing with personal brand stories. They need a memorable twist.

Having a strong personal brand is especially important today when many people have multiple careers over a lifetime or want to look for new opportunities within the same company. Millennial candidates want to work for companies run by leaders who share their personal missions – who have messages they believe in. So, a strong personal brand is also an important recruiting tool.

In my own case, my passion for branding and the seeds of my own unique personal brand were planted at a very young age. It all began when I was eight years old growing up in the 70s in the beautiful seaside town of Marblehead, Massachusetts. I was a happy little girl, but one thing was missing. I desperately wanted a pet – a dog, or cat to call my own. Unfortunately, my older brother was allergic to pet fur, so an animal was out of the question. But even very young, I did not like taking no for an answer. I was always looking for creative ways to solve a problem.

So, I went into our backyard garden, got a rock, put it in an empty Cool Whip plastic container with a few blades of grass for nourishment, poked a few holes in the lid for the rock to breathe and… voilà, instant pet rock. My parents looked at me and my new "pet" kind of funny. They wouldn't realize I was a branding genius until a few years later when the "official" pet rock was launched and made its creator a millionaire. Gary Dahl, an advertising executive from California, was sitting in a bar listening to friends complain about their pets and how they needed to be constantly walked and fed. He got the idea of creating the perfect no-maintenance pet. This led to the idea of selling Pet Rocks to people, complete with instructions.

This is a personal brand story that I often tell when speaking to groups of entrepreneurs or senior executives. It has several important messages about branding and the benefits of thinking outside of the box to create fresh solutions. What is your "pet rock" story? How can you leverage your unique history and experiences to stand out and be seen as the leader you are called to be?

Her Quote

"For a strong personal brand, you need to find your unique twist – and build a plan to stand out."
– Julie Cottineau

Advice for Her

I have had the pleasure of working with supermodel and entrepreneur Tyra Banks, both as a brand coaching client and as a guest lecturer in a class she co-created for Stanford Graduate School of Business called #ProjectYou on personal branding. One of Tyra's favorite quotes is "It's not enough to be perfect, you need to be different." Whether vying for a modeling contract or your next promotion, it is important that people get a sense of who you are – not just your credentials and accomplishments, but what makes you unique and uniquely qualified to lead.

Many women confuse their personal brand with their personality. While they are definitely related, a personal brand is a more crafted and curated presentation. It should feel authentic to who you are, but it needs to be managed. It's not a "take me as I am", warts and all account of your life. It's an edited, crafted and polished story that helps people quickly and clearly get what is special about you, and why they should want to support you as a leader. If you are curating the content and photos you post on social media, choosing those that present you as you want to be seen by the world – not just your appearance but also your interests – then you are already engaging in personal branding.

Whether you like it or not, we all have personal brands. Your personal brand walks into a room before you and hangs around after you've left. It is how people describe you when you are not around. Not just your job function or what you get done in your company, but what it's like to work with you, the "special sauce" you bring to each project, and your leadership style.

Action Steps for Her

Here are three action steps you can take to build a stronger and more unique personal brand:

1. **Twist with people you admire.** A great way to be inspired to tell your own story with a twist is to study the personal brands of people you admire. Note what makes them different and engaging and see how you can apply those storytelling lessons to your own brand.

    One famous brand that has influenced my own story is the chef Rachael Ray, even though I have no interest in or real talent for cooking. Despite my lack of culinary skills, I have always admired Rachael Ray. I like how she has set herself apart from the other more serious, and often intimidating, male chefs in her milieu. When she cooks, she is very casual, engaging and practical. For example, she might say: "The recipe calls for shallots, but if you have a plain old onion, that's just as good." I like how she calls her cooking magazine "Every Day with Rachael Ray." I think her twist is that she takes cooking off its pedestal and makes it fun, relatable and approachable. Early on, when creating my own brand consulting firm, BrandTwist, and my Brand School for entrepreneurs, I decided I was going to channel Rachael. I made sure all of my workshops were engaging and the "recipes" for creating great branding solutions were fun and easy to follow. This helped me stand out from the crowd of other branding experts.

2. **Twist with your personal passions.** Too often women feel that we need to separate our personal and professional lives. But I believe that twisting your personal passions with your professional capabilities can lead to a more memorable personal brand. For example, I had a student in my Brand School who was a high-end kitchen designer. Her work was fabulous and she was recognized with several awards, but she was having trouble standing out in a market crowded with talented (and also award-winning) designers. We decided to step up her branding by twisting in one of her personal passions – ballroom dancing. We explored all of the common skills needed to be successful as both a kitchen designer and an amateur dancer and

there were so many: a commitment to partnership, the ability to move through spaces with grace and fluidity, the skill of breaking large or complicated endeavors into smaller, more understandable steps. She explored these concepts and re-branded her business as "Kitchen Choreography." Her clients loved this concept, she integrated her passion for dance in a more interesting "About Me" section of her website, and her business grew by leaps and bounds.

3. **Create a personal brand plan.** Once you know what you want to stand for and how you want to stand out, the trick is then to identify a plan to get there. Most executives have business plans for their company's brands, but you need a personal brand plan as well. The first step in creating an effective personal brand plan is outlining what you want to be known for and picking values that transcend any single job position. For example, being known for your business acumen instead of for just being a great accountant. The former allows you more flexibility in your career and could open up more opportunities. Or developing a reputation as a strong creative problem-solver, not just someone who is great at producing a good TV spot. Next you need to create concrete action steps to help you close the gap between where you are now and how you wish to be perceived in the future. This might be taking a class, finding a mentor, or proposing volunteering for projects that will help you stretch. I recommend keeping this plan to three objectives, one key action to meet each objective and then checking in

on your plan (perhaps with an accountability partner) every three months to monitor your progress.

Remember, a strong personal brand can be a powerful driver of business and leadership success. But a strong personal brand doesn't just organically develop as part of your personality. It requires attention, aspirations, and adjustments – and above all a twist!

JULIE COTTINEAU

UNITED STATES

Julie Cottineau is a global branding expert, CEO and Founder of BrandTwist, and creator and Dean of her own Brand School. She is the former VP of Brand for Richard Branson's Virgin Group, has held senior agency positions in multiple countries and is the proud recipient of the Business Visionaries Best Business Consultant award.

Julie is passionate about helping businesses, non-profits, and entrepreneurs TWIST their personal and corporate brands to stand out in crowded markets. She is the author of the best-selling book *TWIST: How Fresh Perspectives Build Breakthrough Brands*. Julie is frequently a commentator in media such as CNN, *Forbes.com*, *Entrepreneur and Authority* Magazine.

Her own life has been filled with magical TWISTS and she currently resides in the beautiful Hudson Valley with her French husband, amazing children, and Teddy the wonder Beagle.

Learn more

Website: www.brandtwist.com

LinkedIn: www.linkedin.com/in/julie-cottineau-75285b3

Twitter: @jcottin

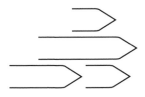

CHAPTER 5

CALLED TO LEAD – CREATIVE LEADER

DIANNE DEVITT

As a young girl, I would firmly place pressure on my tightly closed eyelids with my fingers and vivid colors would appear. Although this act was not popular with my teachers, it symbolized my life's calling as a creative visionary.

As the daughter of a New York City detective and homemaker, my parents instilled in us to "have a skill." This led to secretarial training that prepared me to work for a company president. Unstoppable to attain my college degree, I worked full-time and attended night school for eight years during which I discovered my passion for theater.

My career and destiny were introduced to me while attending a hospitality tradeshow, where I met my future employer and the world of meetings and events. Working tirelessly, and ultimately forming my own company, I did not see that I was a pioneer in an emergent industry. I just did. I constantly sought to learn and became involved with two trade associations that progressed into a Presidential position of the NYC chapters of ILEA and MPI.

During the 2008 financial crash, I lost it all. I was divorced, moved, and became caregiver for my mother. This gave me the time to write my book. In 2009, I wished upon the full moon for something big and subsequently received an opportunity to plan the 40th anniversary event for MIT for Apollo 11. Although eight years of obstacles dared me to survive, I never lost my ability to look ahead. I practiced my yoga and structured the day by doing varied tasks to keep my discipline and focus. Hope and faith gave me the strength to accept the valley I was in and courage to look forward.

Reflecting on high school, I knew that I wanted to make a difference, contribute, and collaborate with others. I did not plan my career path; I trusted my intuition and vision to define me as a storyteller and work with others to help them see what they could not see for themselves.

My career escalated because of what others saw in me and how they encouraged me. Now, I embrace supporting others to see their full potential. Always be open to colorful possibilities, and never forget to wish upon the full moon.

Her Quote

"Creativity is power. Listening to that little voice in your head when you have an idea, not understanding why, but trusting in yourself and having faith in yourself that the idea will work when others struggle to grasp it. Creativity is the voice in your soul telling you to believe in what you think." – Dianne Devitt

This quote came to me at a time when I had to convince myself that *I* was creative. I had designed and taught an extremely successful college-level class on creative thinking for live engagement and was now experiencing rejections and postponements to launch a workshop and certificate program on the same topics. Here I was, the one person others contacted for an idea, solution, or insight, now doubting that my ideas, concepts, visions had merit, and were not good enough. The person who wrote a book on creativity was having what I referred to as my "Picasso Blue" period – a time that I thought selling the concept of creative thinking was not what companies needed.

In hindsight, I realize that the reason I was going through this period was attributed to a few things: the audience I was targeting were *not* creative thinkers who could share the same vision, my concepts were ahead of the curve and the content had to be packaged in such a way to reach the target audience. The timing was not right, as I had not yet connected with the person or entity who would open the door and appreciate my work and understand how it would inspire and help others. I never gave up and finally made an agreement with a leading media company to partner with me to sponsor the events.

The lesson I will always remember is that tenacity is a good mate for creativity, as true creative visions and ideas need the doggedness to stay focused and discipline to bring them to fruition. That, and realizing that being understood as a creative is not always a language other people speak.

Advice for Her

I would like to manufacture a multi-colored pill filled with all the advice of inspirational, historic, and iconic figures in the world and have it readily available to digest at any time. The question is, would I take it at a time when I would be receptive to specific advice or risk losing the wisdom of the ages? In my experience, I have benefitted from advice only when I have been open and willing to receive it. I also learned to not give advice *without being asked for it.*

To me, advice is different from opinions and the "shoulds." I laughed at learning the expression, *"Don't should me."* When coaching or teaching individuals to be more creative, one needs to understand that people all see things from different perspectives and rarely see things "as you see them." By using illustrations and examples I can convey my perspective and various aspects of creativity concepts. It also helps to understand how others think and what their background is when teaching or coaching. If my students believe that I care about them or have a vested interest in their wellbeing, I find I am more successful than when I just deliver information.

Recently I spoke with an astute 30-something woman who notified me that she did not need advice, that she was "adulting." With endearment, I nodded and thought to myself, *"Funny, it wasn't until I became an adult that I searched for advice from as many available sources."* In business, constructive feedback can be a valuable gift.

The best advice I was given was to *Listen and Lead.* In my enthusiasm and with all good intentions, I would often spatter out witticisms, creative ideas or finish a sentence halfway because I believed I knew the thought. How could I? In my leadership positions, I learned that every word I speak resonates and that intentionally listening more enables me to collect information, better understand the root of other people's thoughts, and verify that my message has been both received and understood.

I am aware of my unique talent to visualize things before others. Therefore, I have learned to understand where the individual is before attempting to take them to where they need to go.

Action Steps for Her

Creativity in the business world is evolving as an intrinsic part of standard operations. Gaining unique perspectives and insights from objective sources is being proven to effectively challenge conventional thinking as was the case of bringing in children to give feedback in the toy industry. Focus on Emotional Intelligence ™ in recent years has been recognized as an important component of a team's success. In today's business world, compassionate leaders who create safe working environments that foster open communication and respect for ideas can lead to amazing company results.

1. **Embrace your inner creative.** When asked, most people do not think they are creative. The fact is that everyone is creative.

2. **Allow others around you to express themselves.** Whether through verbal communication, idea boxes, graffiti boards, or any other means.

3. **Learn to illustrate your ideas and concepts in bite-size pieces.** Most people are overwhelmed when creative people bombard them with too many ideas at one time. Presenting creative options and solutions takes a step-by-step approach to allow people to digest and process concepts. Plant ideas and let them germinate and grow.

4. **Exercise your creative brain.** Just like we do physical exercise, we need to do mental and creative exercises to maximize our brain functionality. Read a magazine from a totally different industry; doodle; set your alarm for different times and change your routine a few times a week.

5. **Introduce a Permission to Play™ environment.** Create a safe and supportive atmosphere that allows free-flowing interaction and engagement.

6. **Get involved.** It is easy to forego physical involvement in masterminds, associations, or foundations. Relationships are formed through human connection and empathy. Extend yourself to be a supportive member to expand yourself and help others.

7. **Retain the services of a creative and innovative professional.** Brainstorm and organize a group facilitation to challenge conventional thinking.

8. **Have courage.** It takes courage to believe in new ideas and face adversity. Don't give up.

Most importantly, have fun and remember that creativity is included at the top of the Maslow's Hierarchy of Needs as part of Self-Actualization. Being your true self and believing in your vision is the fuel to drive results.

DIANNE DEVITT

UNITED STATES

Dianne has a prestigious track record as an industry leader and pioneer in the global meetings and events industry. Known as an expert in communicating through innovative solutions, she authored *What Color is Your Event?*, a resource for creative thinking.

For nearly three decades, Dianne owned a premier event agency, The DND Group. The agency offered a wide spectrum of services for executive level events and large-scale productions for CEOs, American Presidents, heads of state, and astronauts. Through her keynote speaking, Dianne has inspired Fortune 100 clients and influenced students as an Adjunct Professor at NYU. Dianne served on executive boards for international associations and received numerous awards and recognitions.

Dianne continues to challenge conventional thinking through her visionary spirit by producing innovative programs, events and workshops to bring people together.

Learn more

Website: www.diannedevitt.com

LinkedIn: www.linkedin.com/in/dianne-budion-devitt-4206458/

Instagram: diannedevitt

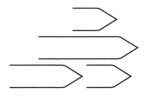

CHAPTER 6

CALLED TO LEAD – VISIONARY LEADER

JENNIFER EINOLF, PCC, NCC, DTM

A paper clip is a loop of wire intended to secure two or more pieces of paper in a coherent stack. To a creative disruptor, a divergent thinker, a paperclip offers a challenge, an opportunity, and a spark that ignites the creative exploration of possibilities. Bend it and it's a fishhook or a pea catapult. Snip it to replace the pin in a hinge.

The mind of the creative disruptor is driven by questions that begin, "What would happen if…" and "There's got to be a way to…" She aggregates ideas and breaks things to fix them. She generates visions – powerful, potent glimpses of a possible future. Ideas flit into view only to be tumbled about by new thoughts, an inexhaustible supply of questions, insights, and solutions.

A creative disruptor's divergent mind is equipped for this and she thrives in the free-for-all of fertile possibilities.

Other minds, the ones who brilliantly execute the plan as described, do not enjoy the tumbled chaos of creative flow. These minds need to see and experience a clear view of a possible future, its potential benefits, and its plan for achievement in order to move to execution.

The world needs both of these minds.

A creative disruptor has a responsibility to design a vision so clear that it is tangible, so necessary that it inspires action, and so persistent that it becomes real. In doing so, we channel the energy generated for creative disruption into the powerful mechanism of visionary leadership.

Typically, visionary leaders face three challenges that test and dare us. We fear ending in regret, leaving our work undone or underperformed. We must overcome the confusion indistinct vision creates for our teams. And we must not allow our passion for the work to obscure the clear connection between self-investment and mission-critical vitality.

Regret is often the only fear a visionary leader is willing to entertain because we, or the visions that drive us, must not end in obscurity. The fears that motivate or paralyze others do not compare to the thought that we might leave important work undone, that we will not realize our potential, or that our mission will not be complete.

This fear of regret is a gift that may fuel our success because it drives us. At the same time, it can further alienate us from those who are differently motivated and drive us to exhaustion. If we focus only on the threat of regret, we lose sight of the possibilities for connection and contribution.

To see our visions realized, we must translate what we see to others. We must design clear vision and develop powerful communication abilities because vision that is indistinct and fuzzy will not inspire and cannot be implemented.

When we are too quick to try to implement a vision without working to clarify it, we risk confusing and exhausting our team. We all need a clear vision of the challenge, the solution, and the plan to get there. The compelling vision requires clarity.

Once the vision is clear, we need powerful skills to transmit it – storytelling, metaphor, vocal and physical skills. The visionary leader is a consummate communicator.

Above all, the visionary leader is not obligated to sacrifice herself to the vision.

We can be so driven by the threat of regret and the demands of the vision that we thoughtlessly engage in sacrificial success. This disconnect obscures the value of self-investment and prevents us from nurturing the vitality necessary to carry our vision to completion. When success comes at the expense of our energy, our health, and our mental agility, we are undermining the very resources we need to sustain that success.

In my work coaching visionary leaders I have witnessed the power of designing a clear vision and communicating it masterfully, while at the same time nurturing the vitality necessary to lead effectively. I design clarity for visionary leadership and livable success.

Her Quote

"As a visionary leader, you have a responsibility to design a clear, compelling vision and communicate it powerfully to others. You are not here to make it happen but to ensure that it happens." – Jennifer Einolf

Advice for Her

In order to channel our creative disruption into visionary leadership, we need to tackle the three challenges – threat of regret, need for clear, catalyzing communication, and nurture of our own instrument of success to build the stamina necessary to see the vision through to completion.

Neutralize the Threat of Regret. Place your focus carefully.

You are not solely responsible for the outcome. You are not responsible for all the work. You have work to do. You will roll up your sleeves and do it. You will not, however, do the work that is better done by others on your team.

You are here not to make it happen but to ensure that it happens. You are the host of the experience and the steward of the space where the work is done. You are here to have the vision, cast it, champion it, and then support the people hooked by it.

It is time to gently nudge any beliefs about have-to into celebrations of get-to. Refine your focus to notice the excitement you feel about the possibilities, not any dread you may feel about falling short. How can you fall short if you get to go farther than you are right now?

To cross the finish line free from regret, you live your life, the one you and only you have been given, in a way that is so coherent with who you are, what you've learned, and what you feel called to create that there is no room for anything else. To cross the finish line free from regret, live that fully. When you do, regret is a lie.

Communicate the Vision and Inspire Movement

A vision must be refined and communicated if it is to have any hope of being realized. This is how the creative disruptor channels her energy into the role of visionary leader. Breaking stuff to make it better is good. Breaking stuff with a team who understands exactly what to break, when to break it and what needs to be built to replace it is the way forward.

Designing clarity relies on the design cycle, a process for fostering creativity and forging solutions. For a vision to become a solution, we must first be clear about the challenge or opportunity that provoked the need to act. The resources and obstacles must be tallied and woven into a statement of the challenge. A plan must be developed and, ideally, tested. The implementation of the plan must be supported. Finally, the process must be evaluated in order to extract lessons for the next iteration of vision to solution.

Because it is a process, the vision does not stay in its initial form. It is allowed to breathe and grow, taking in new input and igniting new creativity. The visionary leader is not demanding a brittle vision be enacted exactly as envisioned. She is inviting her community to realize the vision fully matured, deeply useful, and often surprising in its complex simplicity.

Our responsibility is to learn to communicate fully and to invest in our skills so that we can invest in our people. We speak, notice how it is received, and then use that awareness to craft even more potent verbal connections. We practice the skills that engage audiences, empower thinkers, and build consensus. We master the ability to utilize language to ensure that ideas are seen, heard and felt to ignite different minds.

Thrive Inside Your Success and Sustain Your Contribution

You will not reach the finish line if you wear yourself away now. The vision is compelling, the work is engaging, the team is in motion – the work can be endless. However, if you do not take care of the instrument that you are, the work will end.

The term self-care sparks resistance, guilt, and annoyance for many. Instead, we make self-investments. The time you invest in care for your energy, function, focus, and heart pays dividends in your vitality, efficiency, effectiveness, and satisfaction.

Livable success is facilitated by careful self-investment in nurturing practices and actions. Your wellbeing matters because you deserve to enjoy your life. Your wellbeing also matters because it is necessary to fuel your contribution.

Your vision, your calling, your impact demand that you shed habits that create sacrificial success and invest instead in livable success.

Action Steps for Her

1. **Challenge your motives.** Explore your beliefs about regret, your hidden rules about what success requires – by journaling, working with a coach, or other practices of constructive self-discovery.

2. **Hone your skills.** Organizations and trainers abound to help you develop powerful communication tools. For instance, consider joining Toastmasters, an international organization which fosters communication and leadership skills.

3. **Take care of yourself.** It is that simple and that hard. What is one habit or practice that would support you more fully? Invest in that.

JENNIFER EINOLF

PCC, NCC, DTM
UNITED STATES

Clarity Coach Jennifer Einolf utilizes her background as a commercial interior designer and a serial entrepreneur to apply solid principles of design thinking and growth facilitation to the art of personal learning, leadership development, and transformation.

Her clients, who include Fortune 200 corporate, higher education, and government leaders, learn to design clarity for visionary leadership and livable success. They earn their clarity, activate learning with action, discover their Prospects of Possibility™ and utilize the Clarity Design Cycle™ in order to live, lead, and connect boldly.

She trained with and is certified by the Newfield Network in the Ontological method of coaching and also holds a Professional Certified Coach certification with the International Coaching Federation. An award-winning speaker, she has earned the distinction of Distinguished Toastmaster.

Learn more

Website: www.boldwhisper.com

LinkedIn: www.linkedin.com/in/jennifereinolf

Twitter: @jennifereinolf

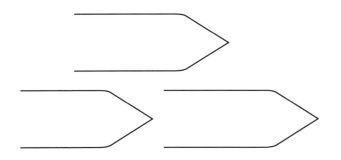

THE POWER OF INFLUENTIAL LEADERSHIP

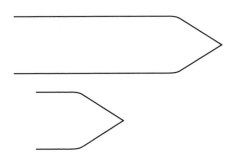

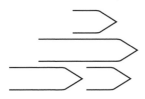

CHAPTER 7

CALLED TO LEAD – NOURISHMENT

DR. CARLA JOHNSTON

My mother's health was always a concern, and she was often sick. She had a myriad of doctors, resulting in differing diagnoses and increased numbers of prescriptions. Unfortunately, as the numbers of medications increased, so did the side effects and symptoms, creating additional health concerns. In between doctor's visits, she began to self-diagnose, adding over-the-counter medications to feel better. At one point, she was taking over 12 medications daily.

I was concerned and began to speak with her about the importance of nutrition, moving her body, and actively practicing stress relief. By incorporating these interventions,

I felt strongly that she could mitigate many of her chronic health challenges. My mother lived a sedentary lifestyle, with poor nutrition habits, and didn't understand the impact this had on her physical and emotional health. She was adamant that if they "were important," her doctors would tell her so. It was time for me to go with her to the doctor.

Leaving her doctor's office, I was shocked. The visit was incredibly short. The only questions asked inquired about new symptoms or concerns since the last appointment. When I interrupted the visit and asked the doctor about their view on nutrition or physical exercise, the response was it was necessary to "eat well and exercise." What did that mean? My mother certainly didn't know what that meant.

Walking to the car, I knew this experience completely changed my life. I knew that there had to be a way to have a bigger conversation than only symptoms and medication, one that focused on Nourishment. I knew that I had to do something.

To this point, my career had primarily been spent as a medical sales representative. I worked with doctors, nurses, and critical care support staff in hospitals. Now, I desired more and explored healthcare through another lens: one that promoted self-care, health behaviors, and the idea of whole-person centered wellness. I felt called to be a leader in a community of practitioners focused on healthcare rather than illness care. This calling was so important to me that I knew I had to act on it. So, in mid-life, I completely shifted my career.

I carefully discerned my business plan and set the following goals:

+ Change from sales representative to practitioner

+ Expand conversations from nutrition to Nourishment

+ Partner with women clients who desire to enhance overall health, including mind, body, and spirit

+ Personalize plans and recommendations based on unique health circumstances to support goals, dreams, and intentions

I created and launched Uniquely Nourishing. To make this life-altering shift, I knew additional education was necessary, and it was essential for me to understand the impact of chronic illness on overall health. I was fascinated by the programs that focused on health challenges and behaviors from various perspectives. It confirmed my belief that we have a fantastic system of medicine, primarily when we can utilize and merge the wisdom of traditional medicine with contemporary evidence-based medicine – it benefits everyone.

It was a risk definitely worth taking. My talks were new to many and began to resonate with my audiences. I started attracting women interested in learning more about my practice and having a larger conversation about their life, not solely food and exercise.

Furthermore, the skills that enabled me to be successful as a sales representative continued to serve me as I began to build my private practice. In addition, the workshops weren't solely on nutrition, calories, diet plans, and exercise; we covered the importance of intention, feeling connected, emotional support, sleep, illness influences, gratitude, movement, meditation, and happiness. I differentiated myself from other practitioners.

There is a wisdom to aging that inspires me and fuels my desire to bring Nourishment programs to those interested in living a health-focused and balanced life. Being focused has allowed me to grow my practice, receive referrals from physicians, and create a second career that brings me joy, fulfillment, and gratification.

Her Quote

"Insert confidence here." – Dr. Carla Johnston

Over the years, I had created and used a simple phrase that had enabled me to move forward when I experienced fear. When I begin to feel unsure or nervous, I say to myself, "Insert confidence here." I quickly remind myself, "You did it before, you can do it again." It usually makes me smile. I imagine that I already have the confidence in my mind's eye, even if I don't feel it at that moment. This phrase is the reminder that believing that I have the confidence allows me to tap into that energy. It has also become a soundbite I share with my clients who use it often.

Fight fear with confidence. Outwardly, it appears that I am confident. I continue to use this phrase to remind myself to remain focused on the tasks at hand and not on my fears. This simple technique has allowed me to continue forward to propel toward new aspirations to new goals. For me, it is second nature to feel fear. I have learned to push through, knowing that it will subside at some point. Usually, when I am attempting something new, it surfaces!

Advice for Her

As a leader, it is essential to continue learning new skills, enhancing current ones, and being willing to stretch yourself, grow, and move forward. "There is always something more to learn, understand, and enhance." Data, circumstances, processes, and people change, so they must be willing and able to adapt. I have witnessed cases where someone has decided that they "like where they are" and do not wish to push forward. It didn't serve them to do so. Some were unable to shift old habits, while others were unable to adapt to new circumstances. It takes effort to keep putting yourself and your ideas out there, having your work judged. It takes practice to continue pushing yourself and your team toward success.

Don't get comfortable. It's crucial to keep in mind that when you arrive at that place when you feel comfortable, it's time to move on. When you begin to feel like everything is going so well, it's time to relax and enjoy it. That can be seductive, staying put and enjoying your success at that point. For many of us, relaxing for too long can lead to an inability to motivate yourself to head toward discomfort, especially when you finally reach a place that you feel great! Things are going well; why change? Moving forward requires effort, risk, and cultivating new skills. The skills that enabled you to achieve success will need to shift to move you upward; continually changing and learning will lead to continued success.

Ask for help. No matter where I have been in my career, I have always been able to ask for help when I felt like I needed guidance. It has and continues to serve me well. Whether an expert, thought leader, or trusted colleague, I find that having feedback from other professionals is essential for growth. At the same time, I make it a priority to help someone else, to lend support to another woman seeking assistance. Always pay it forward. Women supporting women is such a fantastic thing!

Advocate for YOU. Whether you are seasoned in your career or have decided to shift your career direction, it is essential to be your own advocate. It is up to you to create your vision. You must cultivate the skills and techniques that will motivate you when you don't feel motivated, support you when you don't feel supported, build your confidence when you feel uncertain, and confirm your power when you feel powerless. Each of us must cultivate the techniques that resonate with us and rely on those that keep us focused when necessary.

Action Steps for Her

It is essential to assess your skills and talents, especially those that are uniquely yours. Having a clear understanding of your gifts is critical for success. This honest self-assessment will allow you to continue cultivating your skills, leading to growth and success.

1. **Surround yourself with leaders and experts that inspire you.** Ask yourself what about them inspires you? What about them has attracted you to their style, their message, their accomplishments? At the same time, it can help to understand the qualities of those leaders that you don't resonate with or find appealing. This exploration will enable you to develop your instincts, vision, and leadership qualities.

2. **Continue to cultivate your curiosity. Curiosity leads to an openness to possibilities and expansiveness.** Surround yourself with other women who are curious, positive, thoughtful, and successful. Negativity is contagious and spreads quickly. By spending time with other like-minded, goal-oriented women, you become part of the collective energy of success.

3. **Lastly, have fun and enjoy the journey!** And yes, I know this sounds cliché. It can quickly become a habit to work hard, forgetting, or not taking time for self-care, resulting in burnout. Spend time in gratitude, recognizing your life's blessings, family, friends, colleagues, and mentors.

DR. CARLA JOHNSTON

UNITED STATES

Dr. Carla Johnston is an award-winning leader, renowned for her extensive knowledge of critical care products and programs. For more than 25 years, she led organizations by providing clinical support and education.

Dr. Johnston lives her passion – advocating for women who are seeking to incorporate health-positive behaviors into balanced lifestyles.

As Founder/CEO, Carla Johnston leads Uniquely Nourishing, offering programs and workshops that support body, mind, and spirit for women by integrating traditional medicine with contemporary evidence-based research.

Dr. Johnston holds a Doctorate in Clinical Nutrition from Maryland University of Integrative Health, an M.S. in Herbal Medicine from Maryland University of Integrative Health, and an M.A. in Applied Sociology from the University of Maryland, Baltimore County. She is a board-certified Clinical Nutrition Specialist and a licensed nutritionist in Maryland.

Learn more

Website: www.drcarlajohnston.com

LinkedIn: www.linkedin.com/in/carla-johnston-0136a772

Twitter: @drcarlajohnston

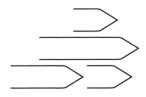

CHAPTER 8

CALLED TO LEAD – THE POWER OF BUILDING RELATIONSHIPS

SHANNA KABATZNICK

I still remember the day my sales manager told me, "You need to network to be successful in your job. The basic formula for success is networking, and it's a numbers game. Meet people, give out business cards, schedule a coffee, learn about what they need, and how you can help." In theory, his method made sense and sounded simple enough until I started doing it.

At my first networking event, I felt out of place, uncomfortable, and disconnected. We were all there to play the "business card coffee game". I thought to myself, "Surely, this is just this one event. Other events will be different."

For the next few weeks, I decided to attend every different kind of networking event I could find to see if my experience changed. It was the same. Sales and transactions were the end game, and I didn't like it. It had nothing to do with listening to others, learning about them, and building relationships. I realized, "If I feel uncomfortable and stressed about networking, surely other women feel the same way."

A burning desire in me insisted that this experience could be bigger, bolder, and more promising. I was called to lead. I didn't know what, when, or how. All I knew was I needed to do it. I began building the blueprint that would encompass everything I felt was missing in "traditional networking."

At the time, I was in the financial services industry, and my market was single mothers or women going through a divorce. Where would I find them? How can I serve them? How can I build relationships with them? I decided to create an event to serve them. I did not know how to create a women's event. I set a date, invited women, and hoped someone would show up. My first event had only a handful of women, and they loved it! They even asked about the next one. The next event brought in more women. By the third or fourth event, there were women that I had never met! Interesting! What was the draw? Why were they here?

I stood back and objectively observed the goings-on. When women left, they felt connected. Women showed up early to meet with each other for an extra 10 minutes to talk. They stayed after the event and made plans to meet for lunch.

What makes effective women's councils, networking events, communities, and women's organizations?

While people at other networking events couldn't wait for the event to be over, women stayed at my events because they wanted more. It was then that we evolved from a networking event to a community building event where women would connect for business, build relationships, and learn from each other.

Women benefitted from joining the community because they experienced:

1. Inclusion

2. Affirmation

3. Connections

4. Safe to be their true selves

These women, like me, needed a place to belong and show their true selves. They looked to me as their leader, and I realized I was called to *be* their leader. Sometimes, we may not see in ourselves what others see in us. When that happens, it's important to acknowledge the possibilities and embrace our newly found role. I now know that leadership is earned by the respect of those around you, the influence and example you set.

Her Quote

"Be FAB! Fearless. Authentic. Bold." — Shanna Kabatznick

Women are strong, we have what it takes, but sometimes fear stops us. As a single mom of two, I had to step out and get over my fear. I had to be the provider, the nurturer, and the caretaker. It was officially the first time I was called to lead. FEARLESS.

I know women are happy when they show their true authentic spirit. When we are authentic, we peel back the layers and show our true selves. We let others know who we really are and attract the people who are like us. There's nothing better than laughing, connecting, and building strong relationships by just being ourselves at home, work, and all around. Giving women safe places to practice their authenticity in professional environments gives them the confidence to be AUTHENTIC.

Bold can sometimes be considered as brash or too strong. Boldness is what moves you forward. When we are called to lead, we need to be bold to share, inspire and connect with others. Being bold allows you to share your ideas, creativity, innovative solutions to challenging and difficult problems. Your boldness comes from serving your organization, teams, and those you care about; be BOLD.

Advice for Her

Life is full of surprises. One thing that is not a surprise is the number of people and relationships you'll build. Building relationships is a crucial component for professional reasons and our personal lives. Take me, at the age of 18, I was sent from Quito-Ecuador to Mississippi State University and did not know a soul! I quickly understood I needed to embrace this opportunity, learn from a different culture, connect with people who did not look like me, or spoke my language, or understood my culture. Looking back, I realize that it was that period in my life that gave me the tools to embrace diversity, celebrate our differences and strengthen relationships.

We do change. However, who we are at our core, our identity, does not change.

Building relationships is all about connecting. To connect, the best approach is always to be authentic. Focus talking points about the other person. People love to talk about themselves. Be quiet, really listen, be genuinely interested, find commonalities and something you can offer to help. When you make the conversation about them, listen more than talk, so they feel heard and want to stay connected. AUTHENTIC.

Also, get comfortable being uncomfortable. Try new things. If you are looking to meet new people, put on a pair of FAB shoes, be bold, and get out there. You know you have something to offer! Walk in a room with confidence. You will find the right connection. Be BOLD.

During your career, you'll have lots of opportunities. Some will not be a good fit; some will be a good fit, and some will be a stretch. When we are stretched is when we are called to be FAB and sometimes called to lead. Do your research and see what's out there, what others are doing that you love, and what things you think you can do better than your competitors. Reach out to other leaders and people you know who can give you solid advice and guidance. Don't try to do it all on your own. Build a network of people you trust that can support your vision. Embrace who you are, and step into your full potential. Take a chance to be FEARLESS.

Most importantly, trust your gut. Believe that if something is nagging at you, there's a reason. Don't be afraid of failing. Be excited about the possibilities of succeeding. When you are called to lead, you do not necessarily know what it looks like, where you are heading, or the end results. All you know is that you need to do it or be haunted by the "what ifs." When you think about leadership, explore different activities and initiatives to create an environment that promotes growth, unity, and strength. When I created that first event, I didn't know the outcome; I didn't know how it would all come together and that a community would be made from an event. I did know that I had to do something that would feed my soul and, in turn, serve other women that needed that as well.

Action Steps for Her

It can be daunting to take the next step in our careers. Here are some ideas on how to start small for a significant return.

1. **Go to an event that sounds interesting to you.** Pick one with a topic or speaker you like and a group of people with common interests. If you're nervous or unsure, try a FAB event first – I promise we'll welcome you with open arms!

2. **Look at ways on how to engage on social media.** If LinkedIn is your platform, start following and commenting on people that are interesting to you. When commenting, provide insight, give value, and make it about them.

3. **Focus on the follow-up.** Be strategic on who you follow up with and why. Remember, you are building a relationship first to learn about them and their needs.

4. **They say, "Do the most challenging task first."** If you are avoiding a client or a prospect, call them first. Take a breath, pick up the phone, smile, and know that you have something useful to offer. Remember, you are not selling but providing an idea, product, or service that they want and need.

5. **Most importantly, have fun, smile, and know that you are FEARLESS, AUTHENTIC, and BOLD!** You can do whatever you set your mind to.

SHANNA KABATZNICK
ECUADOR / UNITED STATES

Shanna Kabatznick, Founder of FABWOMEN, is a speaker, author and trainer who leads an international organization for women's personal and professional development as individuals, team members, and leaders.

Today, Shanna continues training and presenting for the insurance, banking, and financial services industries. Her high energy and magnetic personality creates an inclusive environment where participants feel connected, empowered and motivated.

With over 20 years' experience as a top producer in male-dominated industries, Shanna was the rare Latina that qualified for Million Dollar Round Table (MDRT) and consistently broke sales records and customer engagement because of her authentic style and ability to build long-lasting relationships.

Shanna has been featured on various news channels, podcasts, and is a published author of *Master the Art of Connecting - 30 Tips to Authentic Conversations.*

Learn more

Website: www.shannak.com

LinkedIn: www.linkedin.com/in/shannakabatznick

Facebook: www.facebook.com/fabwomen.rva

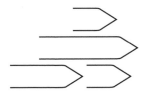

CHAPTER 9

CALLED TO LEAD – BE THE TRIGGER FOR THE CHANGE

ULRIKE AICHHORN, MAS, MTD, CSP

Women, do you know how much power we have in this world? We are an immense sales force and buying force in this world, and marketers and businesses don't even know the power we have!

"80% of purchasing decisions are made by women!"
– Boston Consulting Group & The Nielsen Company

When it comes to marketing, recruitment, and sales in corporations worldwide, traditionally, men have been the majority decision-makers. "Pink it and shrink it" was their approach to enticing the feminine persuasion to buy, buy, buy. Not anymore. We have the power! Korn Ferry shared, "Women hold about 50% of all managerial and professional positions in the United States and account for 41% of employees with authority to make purchasing decisions. In Asia, 31% of management roles are held by women, and more than half of the countries in Europe have similar numbers."

Like all consumers, trust, respect, mindfulness, and honesty are necessary to attract a target group with a brand. Women have the money and have the power to decide how to spend. As long as we stand by our needs, educate others, and express ourselves boldly as company leaders or women consumers, we can trigger the change.

This shift isn't about designing female products or creating a one-off campaign for women. It's not about short-cut events, lots of prosecco, shoes, and pink glitter. We need to say goodbye to stereotypes! As leaders, we are called to initiate change and think outside the box. The best approach for change is for it to start internally, within the heart of the corporation and in every employee's mind. Every division must be involved, including CEO, HR, marketing, sales, after-sales service, with a specifically designed strategy plan to win the female target group.

Just like increasing gender diversity in the C-Suite, we need to use our feminine mystique to turn businesses upside down to learn to sell quality products that are needed *and* desired by us, not the outcome of some "thrown together idea in the middle of the night" brainstorm. Besides, we like many colors other than pink! Yes?

Organizations that serve consumers need to have specific information in order to serve us well. It's our responsibility to step up and make them aware of our needs, our wants.

While waiting in a dealership to see a newly launched SUV, a salesman came toward me and said: "Women cars (the small and cheap ones) are over there." I love big cars with horsepower, so I was pretty annoyed. He failed to ask about my needs and favorites but wanted to impose his opinion on me. I guess you know my answer: "Sorry but I will buy my car at another place. You blew it within the first 10 seconds."

Why should we care? Women are consumers, employees, leaders, mothers, partners, social program supporters 24 hours a day, seven days a week. International surveys show the significance of these decision-makers, but many companies, whatever their size, don't capture the number of possibilities realized with female customers.

Brand loyalty and satisfied customer experience is the shift of focus for businesses everywhere, especially to "win over" women.

A businesswoman booked a trip from Europe to New York. The travel agent recognized that the woman was traveling for business and bringing her child. The agent's goal was to give the best service possible. She found a hotel near a playground with contact information for two doctors and babysitting services. This travel agent went the "extra mile." Cha-ching – can you hear your rewards ring? When the businesswoman gets home, she tells her family, her friends, everyone. By going the extra mile, the travel agent increased brand loyalty and earned referrals.

*The agent recognized the businesswoman's needs beyond the requested flight. She increased sales knowing her customer's needs because she asked to uncover the woman's needs as both a businesswoman **and** a mother.*

Her Quote

"Be the Trigger for the Change!" – Ulrike Aichhorn

As women, we need to use our power to guide companies to prepare for the world's largest consumer group. As self-confident customers, we influence how organizations treat women and how sales, marketing, and processes positively engage women. Voicing our needs and wants is critically important to swing the pendulum in the opposite direction for the diversity of women to be recognized.

Advice for Her

A change in the culture of serving women clientele is in order. Working from within organizations will require sustainable and credible efforts for the long haul.

A banking institute close to Salzburg was courageous enough to create a genius marketing approach that attracted more new women customers than they ever anticipated. I was the consultant and speaker for this campaign focused on "The Self-Confident Woman." It was necessary to work on the bank's message by avoiding typical analyst's presentations with facts and figures but to be focused on benefitting the women by really acknowledging support for them in their different roles. The bank decided to go "the extra mile" when investing money for a forum for women to learn more about self-confidence, to talk to other women and to create a community. The event sold out. The CEO heard about the success, they booked a second campaign and invited me to speak again. Word of mouth worked again, and it sold out… again.

It goes to show that including women in marketing plans and initiatives causes change to occur. We can do a lot to create awareness in business and marketing; when an organization works from the internal structure through to the external, culture shifts. There are so many possibilities.

Companies need to:

✦ Understand how women want to be treated as customers

✦ Honor special requests

✦ Find out how they can contribute an "extra mile" to their products/services

Women need to:

✦ Speak out loud on how they want to be treated

✦ Report direct feedback to companies

✦ Support companies learning how to attract women

✦ Spread the word about women-supported organizations to build their business

Action Steps for Her

A while back, a car company ran an advertising campaign that showed one pink high-heeled shoe and stated, "All women wear pink." Then, it showed a pink car that you could win. A bit incensed, I ran a survey with 20 people and asked men, women, friends, and my sales contact in the car dealership about what they thought of the ad. All of them replied, "Oh my goodness, that cannot be true. Who the hell wants to win a pink car?"

At the urging of my sales contact, I provided feedback to the marketing division in Vienna, the capital of Austria. That afternoon the woman who was responsible for this pink shoe/car campaign called me.

She shared with me that it was her idea because she really loves pink. "What about the other 95 percent?" Puzzled, she didn't understand. I shared with her the results of my short survey about her campaign. I cautioned her that she is going to lose female clients.

She asked me for suggestions. I thought this was her job? I recommended an eight-step campaign. The message of these two campaigns were complete opposites. The dealer was "all women love pink" vs. "women are the most colorful target group."

I recommended the following ad campaign to show the diversity of women and our many, many roles.

- ✦ Day 1 – Pink car for the "pink women"
- ✦ Day 2 – Family van for mommies

- ✦ Day 3 – Station wagon for the DIY women
- ✦ Day 4 – SUV Sport to drive for a mountain bike tour
- ✦ Day 5 – Limo for the businesswoman
- ✦ Day 6 – Small car to find parking place in the city
- ✦ Day 7 – Convertible – have fun and enjoy the sun
- ✦ Day 8 – Sports car – enjoy speed and suspension

Did you find your favorite? Or would you need more than one to handle your roles? When we as leaders, buyers, marketers, consumers open the lens to see how businesses really can serve women, it really isn't that difficult. People are loyal to the brands that serve them.

Here are some additional steps we can take to trigger the change!

As an Executive Woman of an Organization

Initiate an internal, organizational Culture Program

- Strategically engage all stakeholders to guarantee the best impact

- Raise awareness of this target group and its diverse needs in every single division

- Teach teams about the do's and don'ts when dealing with women as customers (this also changes the internal gender behavior as well)

- Develop culture and communication strategies to prepare for the external program

Follow with an External Program "Image & Trust"

- Appreciate the very individual and diverse needs of female customers

- Empower your company and take the lead

- Inspire existing customers

- If women trust, they are loyal and the best multipliers

As a Woman Consumer

- Companies need your strong voice and your feedback

- Share your experiences with other women to help them avoid wasting time and money with their buying decisions

- Share it with the company itself: tell your story, provide ideas for improvement

Be the Trigger for the Change!

ULRIKE AICHHORN

MAS, MTD, CSP
AUSTRIA

Professional speaker and consultant, Ulrike Aichhorn, MAS, MTD, CSP, is a specialist for marketing strategies and initiatives dedicated to the female buyer in the real estate, finance and automotive industries. With 12 years of corporate management experience and more than two decades of consulting, Ulrike commands the attention of marketing and sales leaders with her strategic program, "Quintuple Your Clientele."

Through her services, she leads executives and organizations to the facts about marketing and sales involving the female buyer persona and she coaches executive women on leadership excellence.

Ulrike is the first Austrian woman to be awarded the CSP Certified Speaking Professional, the highest international speaker designation; she has earned two Master's degrees in organizational development and business training; and is a Certified Process Manager and Lead Quality Auditor.

Learn more

Website: www.die-aichhorn.com

LinkedIn: www.linkedin.com/in/dieaichhorn

Facebook: www.facebook.com/dieaichhorn.at

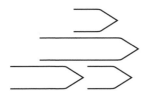

CHAPTER 10

CALLED TO LEAD – CROSS-CULTURAL LEADERSHIP

DIANA WATSON, MA, MS, DTM

I want to provide simple insight to help you succeed if you work overseas with a team, do virtual work globally, or even perform work in another culture within your own country.

I was a little Black girl with long ponytails and a curious obsession with globes and encyclopedias in the 1970s. I grew up in a household of dichotomies. My father used his charm and Philadelphia street-smarts to excel in every leadership position he enthusiastically undertook. In contrast, my mother preferred the personal comfort of suburban life and resisted leadership until her sixties when she had to handle her parents' affairs as the eldest.

As a child, my mother often said, "Diana, don't take on any extra responsibility. [Leadership] is hard, underappreciated work, and people disappoint you." She was persuasive, so I was happy to languish in my mother's "easier life, no strife" camp for many years. But one day, my heart clearly said, "It's time to lead."

That day came when I decided whether to run for president of a Toastmasters' Club in Taiwan in 2010. During this time, the Taiwanese economy was devastated, and the club was dying. I felt an inner yearning to serve because I had ideas that I knew would help. But clubs at that time were reserved for elite members of Taiwanese society. To run for president required three unspoken criteria: serve as an officer before running for president, speak Mandarin, and be rich. I lacked all three, so I ditched the idea.

One day I asked my club mentor, "I think I want to be an officer. Which one should I choose?" She quickly responded, "Why don't you run for president?" I was too shy to admit to her I wanted that all along, but I still didn't feel confident. So, I said, "The members won't accept me. My Chinese is crappy, I haven't been an officer before, and I'm broke!"

"So what! Let me talk to the members," she said. Not surprisingly, many weren't supportive. But my mentor believed in me and convinced them to give me a try. They admittedly had nothing to lose since no one else wanted the role.

Immediately I had to make very unpopular, authoritative decisions such as moving the venue from a fancy hotel to a much cheaper, windowless bank basement. Membership dipped to the lowest levels since the club began 25 years prior. I often lay awake at night, scared and unsure of my decisions.

In a few months, I slowly built alliances with members and earned their trust. I integrated all the Mandarin I knew into every conversation and intentionally praised my officers during meetings. I showed up to members' strenuous outdoor excursions and attended their children's birthday parties. And the more I showed up, the more my members supported me and my decisions. I made history as the youngest and first foreign female president of any Toastmasters' Club in Taiwan. Today the club is strong, has earned numerous speaking and leadership awards, and is still in the windowless bank basement!

When challenged when leading in a culture different from your own, here are some pointers that will help you be effective.

Her Quote

"It's not about being right; it's about doing the right thing at the right time." – Diana Watson

Advice for Her

1. Be a "Speaking Seed." I created the term "Speaking Seed" to define a person willing to learn the local

language to share information or experiences with others and promote better cross-cultural understanding and relationships.

Now you don't have to become an advanced or near-native speaker. But nothing trumps learning the language if you want to build alliances, encourage commitment to action, and build trust. Learning the language is as important, if not more so, than the project or work you're there to do.

Another reason to be a Speaking Seed is for your career security. In most overseas assignments, companies will pair you with a local person who acts as your cultural liaison and interpreter. Because this individual controls the information you receive, they have a lot of power over whether your assignment succeeds or fails. Knowing the language gives you more control. It will also enable you to receive critical insight from various people, including colleagues and local acquaintances. Also, do you want your liaison attached to your hip the entire time?

But listening is an even more critical communication skill than speaking. You might be asking how I know so much about Taiwanese culture. I do because Taiwanese people are willing to share their culture with me. After all, I respect their language, and I'm willing to really listen.

2. Never "throw anyone under the bus." In most cultures, people hate to lose face, so be sure not to call

them out at a meeting. If you have a problem with an employee, don't go to their boss and don't confront them directly either. Handling misconduct or inaction at work typically requires a subtle touch — delegate this to your cultural liaison. If it's a colleague with whom you have a relationship or don't have a liaison, speak gently to your teammate in private and send a follow-up email thanking them for their understanding and commitment to the work, even if they are lazy or incompetent.

In the end, attitude, not competence, is everything. If you cause a critical person on your team to lose face, your reputation will quickly plummet, and your assignment will likely fail. Be patient and let them float along.

Leading cross-cultural teams requires extra patience. You must be the learner, the motivator, the empathizer, the promoter, and the transformer, in addition to being the leader. Remember, you are the guest, and you have everything to lose. *It's not about being right; it's about doing the right thing at the right time.*

3. Show up. Show up to Happy Hour even if you're exhausted after a long work week. Show up for the christening of an employee's baby, even if it takes your whole free Saturday. Show up for a subordinate's choir performance even if she sings like a rooster. Whenever you're invited to an event, move heaven and earth to be there.

Action Steps for Her

If you volunteer or find yourself in a cross-cultural leadership position, know that you will embark on a challenging yet life-changing experience. But to reap the rewards, you simply cannot be lazy, uninterested, or stubborn. It would be best if you embraced uncertainty and curiosity. These steps will help you succeed as a cross-cultural leader:

1. **Take a personality test.** You need an objective view of your character before you work in another culture. To appreciate and gain the most out of the experience, you would ideally be agreeable, tenacious, extroverted, open to new experiences, and able to handle ambiguity. If you lack these traits, seek out experiences to help you practice them and grow.

2. **Learn as much information about your new colleagues' cultures from as many sources as possible before you start.** If you are a senior manager in an international firm with teams spanning multiple continents, doing that research will indeed be challenging. But I argue that understanding them is critical for your project's success.

3. **Establish a support system.** You should have a minimum of two personal alliances if you live in a foreign country or one if you are only communicating with people in foreign locations. With the growth of virtual work, you have to put in extra effort to connect with people and build your social capital to make informed decisions.

4. **Perfect your communication skills.** Practice your written and oral communication skills as much as possible. If you hate public speaking, practice it anyway. Effective leadership mandates it.

5. **Ensure your hard skills are excellent.** There is more than enough pressure to acclimate to a new place in cross-cultural assignments and learn a new culture above and beyond doing your job. You want to make sure that you prepare for the task at hand. The other pressures you'll face will challenge you so much that training new teams and performing rudimentary tasks will require massive amounts of your time and energy in your new location.

6. **Support your team unwaveringly.** Even if you think your teammates are idiots or jerks, staunchly defend them and come to their rescue when they need help. Share the load when they fall behind and bear the responsibility when they mess up. They will usually respond to your loyalty with appreciation, and this will strengthen team spirit.

No other category of leadership is as challenging and fulfilling – and yet also the least financially rewarding! But money doesn't drive cross-cultural leaders. I thrive with differences and embrace multiple truths. Nothing gives me a bigger high than to create impactful visions, make challenging decisions, and implement meaningful actions in a foreign country. So, if you're offered a cross-cultural opportunity – go for it!

DIANA WATSON

MA, MS, DTM
TAIWAN

"Am I Strange?" is Diana Watson's most renowned presentation with over one million views within two weeks. As a bilingual professional, Diana also presents in Mandarin, and this one video transformed how the world views Black people who speak Chinese.

A four-time Taiwan Toastmasters English and Mandarin national speaking champion, cultural immersion expert and highly regarded author, Diana has earned numerous Toastmasters leadership awards and is recognized as the go-to expert who leads individuals and organizations on how to effectively become immersed in new cultures with her training programs on cross-cultural leadership, foreign language public speaking, and cultural intelligence.

Diana equips clients on how to obtain critical knowledge to drive profitable initiatives that positively impact the local culture. Diana's first book, *The Speaking Seed: Secrets to Successful Foreign Language Public Speaking*, is the first book ever dedicated to foreign language public speaking.

Learn more

Website: www.dianawatson.net

LinkedIn: www.linkedin.com/in/watsondiana

Twitter: @thespeakingseed

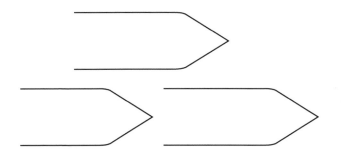

THE POWER OF EMOTIONS AND THE MIND IN LEADERSHIP

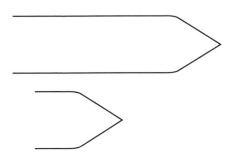

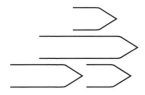

CHAPTER 11

CALLED TO LEAD – LEADING UNEXPECTEDLY IN A CRISIS

CATHERINE WOODHOUSE, MD

Leadership inherently involves emergencies and utter catastrophes. They're inevitable. As such, good leaders plan and prepare for them in advance. But what happens when a crisis strikes and you're suddenly tasked to lead in a role you've never held before? A simple mnemonic can help you navigate acute leadership successfully, and you can glean deeper insight from your experience.

"Code Blue, Room 552," blares the hospital loudspeaker at 2:00 AM. "Code Blue, Room 552." The blue pager clipped on the waistband of Dr. Smith, the newly minted second-year internal medicine resident, buzzes violently. She jumps out of her bed in the call room and sprints up the three flights of stairs. Bursting breathlessly out of the stairwell, she joins four other staff racing in lockstep to the beside of a gray-haired older woman, gray-faced and limp, being rolled on her side by a nurse deftly placing a CPR board underneath her back. Another nurse steers a bright red metal crash cart into the room, bristling heavily with various monitors, oxygen masks, and medications.

The resident descends upon the patient who is clearly not breathing and pulseless. In her white coat, it is understood to both herself and the six other team members that she is the only physician in the room.

Although all the code team members are trained in advanced life support, each face is turned expectantly to her for direction. For leadership. This is her very first time running a code all alone, surrounded by strangers. But the gray woman is dying.

"I'm Dr. Smith," she announces bravely, trying to hide her insecurity. "Let's start CPR."

There's no time for other introductions or pleasantries. Dr. Smith gestures as deferentially as she can toward each responder in turn.

"Please take the airway. You start chest compressions. I need you on the defibrillator. Will you check the IV and prepare to give meds? And will you pull up the patient's chart? Will you keep time? Thank you, everyone."

The resuscitation dance begins. Pure oxygen is hand-squeezed into the patient's lungs. Her heart is compressed and stunned with electrical shocks as medications are given to coax back a heartbeat. Dr. Smith asks the patient's nurse about her history and does a chart review, considering the possible reasons this gray-haired woman went into cardiac arrest, and trying to treat them in turn.

Six minutes of looped interventions pass. Dr. Smith asks, "Does anyone have any other ideas?" Her team does not, but she's witnessed well-run codes before when involving the whole team yielded critical benefit. Three more minutes of tense, steady work click by. Suddenly one of the nurses yells, "I got a pulse!" All goes still. Dr. Smith silently confirms there is indeed a weak, thready pulse at the woman's neck. The team backs away for a moment, exhaling into a collective smile. Someone claps. Special infusions are started, and the no-longer gray woman is whisked away to the ICU.

Sometimes you are forced to lead in an emergency on the fly, with millions of dollars and hundreds of jobs on the line, or with your very own job at stake. You're suddenly called upon to step forward on behalf of your team and be on the hook for the success of the entire project. Sure, your teammates have their own roles to play. But it is now up to you alone to step forward courageously and lead, ready or not.

Her Quote

"Face crisis like a bad haircut. No matter how awful it looks now, you know it'll all grow back eventually."
– Dr. Catherine Woodhouse

Advice for Her

When this role is thrust upon you, you can lead urgently without imploding or exploding. You can stand firmly and not only carry the moment but carry it with confidence. You can use the same steps that comprise an effective emergency Code Blue resuscitation by remembering your A-B-Cs: Assign, Begin, and Connect.

Action Steps for Her

First, Assign roles immediately. You simply cannot handle a crisis alone. Having people in place allows you to take a 30,000-foot view of what's going on. It's extremely challenging to direct a resuscitation and give chest compressions at the same time. Of course, in an emergency you don't always have enough people and may have to do multiple jobs yourself as the leader.

But if you are able to step back just a wee bit, you can better see where you're doing well, where you're stretched thinly, and where you have actual holes. You're able to ask more detailed questions. Why did this patient's heart stop? What is really happening with this merger? What else can we do to provide the client value above just responding to this emergency? What do we still need resource-wise?

You may not know your people intimately at the start of a crisis, but you will. The people around you are your greatest asset. Stay alert to their status during the work and be prepared to switch their roles if they're struggling. The code team member doing vigorous chest compressions will fatigue after a minute or two, which exhausts and depletes them as well as compromises the patient's circulation. As a leader it's critical to stay vigilant for people who are struggling and assign them to another role to preserve the mission and their wellbeing.

Secondly, Begin. Lead. Jump in, feet first. Be the excellent leader you've just been elected to be. Just do the thing. It may not be pretty or smooth at first, but trust that you will certainly find your footing, and afterward your rhythm. The hardest part is often starting, gaining momentum. And as you begin, never be too proud to ask for input. Your team is smart. Involve your people. You are equals, just with different roles. Soliciting input can be humbling, but it will make the outcome better for everyone involved and lead to a much higher chance of success.

Regarding success, decide at the outset what success will look like for you and your team as you act. About 70% of hospital resuscitations successfully revive the heart, but only 20% of those patients ultimately survive to make it back home. If code teams made survival to discharge their sole criterion of success, they would feel like utter failures 80% of the time. The truth is that people whose hearts and breathing stop already have serious bodily dysfunction and can die regardless of a code team's best efforts. Bottom line: some things are irreversible. The expected success of resuscitation is not only a heartbeat, but above all that the team does their absolute best. If their own mothers were being resuscitated, each member of the team would use every ounce of knowledge, skill, and strength they possessed in their mom's time of need.

In your emergency, are you doing your utmost best with all the collective knowledge, skill, and resources you have? Are you accurately assessing which situations might be irreversible and directing your efforts elsewhere? Or might you be giving up too soon?

If you choose the success metric of you and your team doing your utmost best, and meet it, graciously accept its fruit. Don't beat yourself up over outcomes that are beyond your power to achieve.

Lastly, Connect. After a resuscitation, doctors meet with the family and team to share what happened, answer questions, and provide heartfelt comfort. And your team needs the same in crisis. Comfort is so critical, yet many leaders don't take any time to do it. Interpersonal connection is chronically undervalued as soft, feminine, and optional.

I must reiterate: your team is your most valuable asset. They're the ones who make the mission possible. Leaders who focus exclusively on the mission or outcome and neglect their teammates suffer loss both in real time and in the future.

Performing under duress is quite stressful and can damage your people's physical, mental, and emotional wellbeing.

Protect your team's wellbeing at all cost. Aggressively seek to understand what they're going through and serve them as best you can. Not only will you enhance the outcome, you will surely forge a strong team through bonds of mutual respect and loyalty by the shared crisis experience. And those bonds will not easily be broken.

Unplanned leadership in a crisis is not easy, and hopefully it is rare. The A-B-Cs of "Code Blue" leadership – Assign, Begin, and Connect – can help you the next time you're tapped to lead in an emergency.

Understand also there is deeper truth inherent in crisis. Consider this: the tempest comes that you might meet it. If it is knocking at your door, both success and growth are possible. You may not understand why – why this crisis, why now, why you. But the sheer developmental potential contained within the crisis is staggering.

A bonus is that emergencies are thankfully self-limited; they come to pass. Exactly like a bad haircut. Don't worry, you will do just fine. All eyes are on you. Shine!

CATHERINE WOODHOUSE

MD
UNITED STATES

Dr. Catherine Woodhouse is a triple board-certified physician in Internal Medicine, Pediatrics, and Bariatric Medicine. As a Commissioned Corps officer of the U.S. Public Health Service, she crisscrossed the country for eight years providing care to medically underserved communities and served in Hurricane Katrina. She subsequently provided coverage in a hospital-based private practice system. She's been a proud professional locum physician for over 20 years.

Dr. Woodhouse authored a medical humor book, *Party Gown: A Doctor's Laughable Advice,* and co-invented a device for wheelchair users to improve their mobility in non-pristine terrain.

A joyful and thriving burnout survivor, she loves helping occupationally stressed women physicians realize their power to create new work. She lives in Atlanta with her wonderful family and is a colossal fan of books, learning, exercise, good food, laughter, and singing loudly in the shower.

Learn more

Website: www.doctorwoodhousespeaks.com

LinkedIn: www.linkedin.com/in/catherinewoodhousemd

Facebook: www.facebook.com/doctorwoodhouse

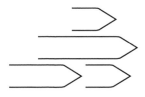

CHAPTER 12

CALLED TO LEAD – MENTAL WELLNESS

DR. BONNIE WIMS

I awoke to the sound of a door slamming with such force that for a minute I thought it was a gunshot. The silence afterward told me my father had left the house, most likely in a drunken rage. Without thinking, I found myself climbing out of bed and walking up the two flights of stairs from my basement bedroom I shared with two of my four sisters. Typically, when all of the shouting and beatings started, I would do all I could to hide and stay small. As the seventh of eight children and just six years old, I was usually successful in just blending into the background until I felt safe enough to disappear to my bedroom or some other place far from the most recent terror. But this night was different, I wanted to see my mother.

"Let's leave," I said softly as I walked into the kitchen. She didn't initially look up. She sat at the kitchen table holding her face in her hands, silently crying. "Please," I said again. Eventually she brought her hands down to reveal tearful, sad and pain-filled eyes. She looked at me with a contrasting sweetness and more than a little condescension. "We can't," she said simply, as if the subject was already closed. I rushed to her, climbed on the chair next to her and touched her arm urgently. "Why not?" I pleaded, feeling my own tears in the back of my throat. Even before she answered I knew we wouldn't be going anywhere. I saw the slumped defeated shoulders and the vacant look of someone who had already given up years before I had come into the world. The option, the choice of a different life was nowhere in her thoughts.

But what I didn't understand then, and perhaps continue to consider in my work as a psychologist today, was the depths of the emotional prison my mother was already in. Even if we had plenty of money (which we didn't), and somewhere else to go (which didn't exist), my mother was not entertaining the choice of leaving her abusive and alcoholic husband. If she had ever given that thought serious consideration, that moment had passed long ago. She was sunk so deep into this life that was not her own, the possibility of another was not even in her sights and most especially not going to be encouraged by an earnest, yet naive six-year-old girl. However, without either of us being aware of it, her denial of my plea to leave this abusive life, to choose a different path, set my own life off on a trajectory of self-discovery, yes, but also one of a laser-focused commitment to try and understand the importance of mental wellness.

Her Quote

"The truth of who you are is not in what you are told or what you are taught, but rather the true nature of you is in what you choose." – Dr. Bonnie Wims

I spoke to my mother later in her life, long after my father had died, about how she felt about her choices and how she understood her role in our traumatic childhood of violence and fear. Her perspective seemed heavy with guilt, defensiveness and excuses. She spoke of doing the best she could, given the circumstances. She spoke of loving this man in spite of his cruel and tormented soul. She remained committed to the idea that she had no choice but to fold herself into his life, his expectations and pain. She wore this idea of no choice like a badge of honor and with this award of self-sacrifice she could rationalize keeping her eight children captive too. But the one thing I don't think she ever realized was that she was not alone and that we were all there to share the burden, even if just for a little while, to support her in a different choice.

In *Man's Search for Meaning*, Viktor Frankl says, "Everything can be taken from a man but one thing: the last of the human freedoms – to choose one's attitude in any given set of circumstances, to choose one's own way."

Although this can feel difficult at times, listening to our true "selves", tapping into our own strength is the only real way to find our own meaning. Allowing our sense of self to be altered, impacted or even destroyed by another person, or life's difficulties and pain, can inflict the greatest damage to our ability to change and grow. If we allow these outer influences to invade our sense of our own possibility and meaning making, our ability to then use that inner strength and power to make good decisions can be squashed or even diminished. Our attitude, our belief in ourselves that lives within us all, needs to be nurtured and listened to, even if we are scared or aren't sure where it will lead us. Much like that six-year-old that was called out of her bed to put a voice to the inner sense of strength and belief that there was another way, our true self is inside us just waiting to be allowed to speak, lead, and to help us find our true meaning.

Advice for Her

Sometimes life is hard, unfair and frequently can scare the confidence right out of us. There are no guarantees in life, but humans by design work to find meaning, and seek connections. We all need to feel validated. That is what is at the heart of our deep yearning: to feel connected, seen, and understood. Without that, we feel adrift, isolated, and depending on our underlying beliefs about ourselves, we can feel shame and blame ourselves for this hollow we feel in our soul.

In therapy sessions with clients, I ask people to put aside what others have said to them, what opinions they may have ingested in their lifetime, or what judgments they have decided to accept. I ask clients to pay attention to their self-talk and to become aware of the destructive way they can have of communicating with themselves. As clients become aware of these internal conversations where they can stoke their worst fears and remember all the pain they have endured, we can begin to understand their worldview and how it was shaped. Our perception of ourselves can feed limiting beliefs and prevent us from feeling capable of choosing a different way. The self-fulfilling prophecy of choosing more pain, sadness, conflict or anger, and then using these choices to confirm our bleak worldview, is the most powerful tool we use and many of us aren't even aware that we do it.

Becoming aware, working to notice the unhelpful conversations we have with ourselves and pushing back against our tendencies to believe the negative messages are all vital steps to understanding how we see ourselves. But it doesn't stop there. The awareness is just the beginning of the journey. Taking active steps to counteract the negativity, insecurity, and doubt is where the real work begins.

Action Steps for Her

The effort to change must be a conscious one. Changing our perspective, understanding our habits and working to alter the unhelpful way we have of relating to the world is challenging. I often compare this work in therapy to altering the course of a large ship on the ocean. Even as the awareness grows and we begin to make changes, the impact on our life can be delayed as we begin to alter the relationship we have to ourselves and our life. If we take into consideration that some of our most damaging thought patterns and traps may have been built in us from childhood, it is understandable that any changes to these habitual patterns can take time.

That being said, the steps I consistently take with clients to support them on this journey are:

1. Examine life choices and be honest about why these choices were made.

2. Get help mirroring your reasons back to you so any self-deception or contradictions can be highlighted and examined.

3. Review helpful and unhelpful thought patterns that are shaped by underlying beliefs.

4. Be patient and kind with yourself, but vigilant. Change can be hard.

Although creating new and healthy ways of seeing ourselves whilst also changing unhelpful and habitual behavioral patterns can be difficult work, the payoff is twofold. Our ability to begin to trust ourselves to make good choices that enhance our life builds on itself as we move from challenge to challenge with a sense of confidence. But lastly, and maybe most important of all, our sense of resilience, the ability to bounce back from a difficulty, begins to grow with each measured and conscious choice we make. Much like the six-year-old that lives in me, I am called to listen intently to what I need and want so that the choices that help me live a fulfilled life are made and honored.

DR. BONNIE WIMS

UNITED STATES

Dr. Bonnie Wims was professionally trained as a Counseling Psychologist in London, England while living in the United Kingdom. While there, she founded her private practice, Wims & Associates, and began working with individuals and couples. It was at this point that she began to clarify her mission to work side by side with individuals who held limited belief in themselves and their potential to live a fulfilled life. In addition to working with clients one-on-one, Dr. Wims has designed workshops and courses on identity and self in a new culture. Upon moving back to the United States, she has continued working online with clients from around the world.

Learn more

Website: www.bonniewims.com

LinkedIn: www.linkedin.com/in/dr-bonnie-wims-psyd-63614930

Twitter: @dr_wims

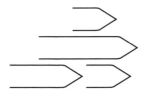

CHAPTER 13

CALLED TO LEAD – BE THE FRIEND NEXT DOOR FOR YOURSELF AND OTHERS

CINDY TSCHOSIK

It was the summer of 2008. My daughter was six and my twin sons were five. I was obsessed with staining our three-year-old deck. Each morning, my friends called to go to the pool. "No, I'm staining my deck." Really? Summer should be fun. I was obsessed, stressed and boring; I cried a lot. My stress level was at the tightest span of a rubber band. Any second, I could snap and shatter.

Knock. Knock. My friend, Dawn, was at the door with glasses of lemonade. Ahhhh. We head to the newly stained deck. It was finally finished, a month later. It was a bit chaotic. The cable guy was on the telephone pole and the kids were frolicking in the yard. I'm crying the ugly cry.

With a listening ear, Dawn empathized with me. She leaned in, "I hope you don't mind me saying this… I think you might be depressed."

"Depressed? What do I have to be depressed about? I have this new house, a great husband, great kids, food on the table, clothes on my back. I don't have any reason to be depressed."

"Cindy, it's not like that. It's not emotional. It's medical. The symptoms for depression are different for everyone. For instance, when I'm struggling, I'm a raging witch with a capital "B.""

Symptoms. That day, my life changed. She was my friend, and she saved my life. I never knew she struggled. Unfortunately, there's still a stigma. However, the more we share and learn, the stigma will lessen.

I thought depression was only crying and staying in bed all day. I didn't think we could be functional *and* depressed. That was shocking. It shouldn't have been a surprise. I was living what I thought was my "new norm." I didn't realize I was no longer myself.

It's a medical disease. It's not something you can shake off. If we have diabetes or high blood pressure, it's necessary to treat it with insulin or medication, perhaps a change in diet and activity level. When you put it that way, why is there such a stigma?

Dawn further shared that once she started medication and talk therapy, she felt more like herself. She made me promise I would see my doctor the next day.

Solutions. After a quick assessment of questions, the doctor confirmed out of the eight different types of depression, I had major depressive disorder. There are also five different major types of anxiety. Who knew? We talked about treatments. Since I had struggled so much for so long, I opted for medication and psychotherapy.

Within three days, the taut rubber band succumbed a little bit. I could breathe a little bit. Within 10 days, I started to feel more like me. I was astonished. Depression. Thank God for Dawn!

Since then, I've been living through depression and then bouts of anxiety. I say "living through" because it's not my companion. It's what I need to monitor, manage, and modify. I've learned, analyzed, and identified a lot about myself and this mental disease that affects 264 million people around the world.

I'm best when I Connect the Dots to the Symptoms, Solutions and Soundbites of Mental Wellness™. When I speak to corporations, organizations, and associations. I'm honored to share my story and solutions because it leads many people to mental wellness.

Her Quote

"Be the Mental Wellness Friend Next Door for Yourself and Others." – Cindy Tschosik

Our days are filled with people, events, responsibilities, and emotions. Mental health challenges can sweep into our life and catch us by surprise. One minute we're fine. Three hours later, our emotions have taken over everything and everyone is at risk for a lightning strike. When we learn more, we do more, and we maintain mental wellness.

I've learned to "categorize" my emotional, psychological, spiritual, and physical states of mental wellness as The 5 Phases of a Storm™:

1. Sunny Skies. All good!

2. White Clouds. Little off.

3. Gray Clouds. Shaking my epicenter.

4. Stormy Clouds. Rocking my epicenter.

5. Spiraling Tornado. Off my epicenter. Suicidal ideations, planning.

When we ward off the storms with Daily Mental Health Checks, we better understand ourselves, and life is definitely sunnier!

Advice for Her

Soundbites. As leaders, we must connect the dots to our own mental wellness, *and* we need to be aware of our employees' mental wellness. But how? When we learn the symptoms and soundbites (in my newsletters at CindyTschosik.com) we can Be the Friend Next Door™ and suggest solutions.

Remember

1. All symptoms present differently in each person.

2. A combination of Mental Health Checks, exercise, good nutrition, sunlight, time with loved ones or pets and a positive mindset can keep the simple blues away and even positively amplify the treatment for any diagnosis. Taking care of *you* and those you care about is what it's all about.

3. Mental health challenges are mental *diseases*. It's not an emotional response. It's a chemical imbalance unbeknownst to you, requiring medical intervention.

4. When mental diseases plague us, we feel like it's our "new norm," stripping us of ourselves. Once treatment, whichever type works for you, is integrated into your life, you'll feel more like you again.

You first

Depression and anxiety are full-body experiences because they settle into our emotional, psychological, spiritual, and physical ecosystems. We can tend to slough it off like it's "the blues" or a "bad day." Here are some soundbites for you to consider:

+ How are you feeling in each of the four ecosystems?

+ Have those feelings lasted two weeks or more?

+ Do you feel like yourself or don't recognize yourself?

Now them

"Them" includes the people that work for you, with you and those you love. Sometimes, as leaders, we feel awkward addressing a "personal" matter. However, you can change or save someone's life. People need us to Be the Friend Next Door™. Whenever someone is behaving differently than normal, and especially in the opposite extreme of their normal, it is a definite sign they are struggling.

Here are some behaviors and soundbites that signal struggles. They can be very casual, sarcastic, humorous, or almost inaudible.

Different Behaviors (Their Symptoms)	Unusual Responses (Their Solutions)	Statements (Their Soundbites)
Oversleeping	Always late to work	"Sorry, just can't get out of bed these days."
Looking unkempt	Avoid face to face conversations; isolate in office	"Not feeling good again."
Decreasing sales / results	Not talking to clients / co-workers	"Well, it is what it is." "Can't deal." "Too much."
Negative attitude when usually positive	Short fuse, isolation, excessive drinking, eating, exercising	"I need a drink." "Stress meal." "I'm running twice a day."

Action Steps for Her

Solutions. There are so many options to support yourself and others.

1. If symptoms have been happening two weeks or more, it's time to see your doctor – today or tomorrow – asap!

2. Add these phone numbers to your favorites list right now:

    *   911 – US Emergency

    *   Suicide Prevention Hotline
        U.S. – 1-800-273-8255

    *   Depression & Substance Abuse Hotline
        U.S. – 1-800-662-4357

    *   Emergency Friends/Relatives

    *   If you live in/travel to different countries, search their emergency number and suicide prevention hotline

3. Three Daily Mental Wellness Checks

    *   Pause

    *   Deep breath... In... Out... 3 x

    *   Check in with your heart and head. How am I feeling? Sunny skies, white clouds, gray clouds, stormy, spiraling tornado?

    *   Why is that?

- What do I need right now? Walk? Quiet time? Deep breathing? Journal? Meditation? Punching bag? My toolbox?

- Repeat until feeling better

- If you can't achieve a better mindset, call friends or emergency personnel

4. Build Your Mental Wellness Toolbox!

- List of favorite activities

- Items that make you smile or bring back a good memory

- Journal

- Positive letters from yourself or others

- Quotes

- List of people to call

5. If you have dark thoughts *like* these listed below, call those numbers you marked as "favorites." You matter, and you deserve a better life.

- I'm worthless

- The world doesn't need me

- My family would be better off without me

- There's only one way to escape this pain

6. If you don't know exactly what to say to get help, start with "I can't be alone right now. I'm having dark thoughts. I need help." You have the courage to do this, and you must. People love you!

7. To learn more about the Symptoms, Soundbites and Solutions™, visit www.CindyTschosik.com

Congratulations! You now know how to Be the Friend Next Door™ for yourself and others. That is what matters – that you do something about it. When we learn more, we do more. These are life skills. Once you recognize and help others recognize how to address these types of challenges, we learn how strong we are and how we can survive and thrive through our mental health challenges. And that is how to Be the Friend Next Door!™

CINDY TSCHOSIK
UNITED STATES

Cindy Tschosik is a certified ghostwriter, professional speaker, and mental wellness advocate.

For more than 25 years, Tschosik held leadership roles in legal, corporate, IT, and nonprofits. In 2013, she launched SoConnected, a full-service marketing firm for business owners and professional speakers.

During a challenging summer in 2008, Tschosik was diagnosed with major depressive disorder. Her journey and her mission came out of her mental wellness journey.

From the laptop, she ghostwrites nonfiction books for mental health professionals, influencers and artists who share their expertise and/or journey to achieve mental wellness.

From the stage, she Connects the Dots to Symptoms, Solutions and Soundbites for Mental Wellness.

With her clients, together, they valiantly inspire others how to achieve mental wellness.

Learn more

Website: www.soconnectedllc.com

LinkedIn: www.linkedin.com/in/cindytschosik

Twitter: @cindytschosik

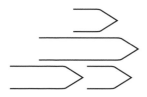

CHAPTER 14

CALLED TO LEAD – MASTERING THE UNDENIABLE POWER OF EMOTIONS

DR. PATRICIA (PAT) BAXTER

We don't always realize we are being called to lead and serve.

I stepped out from behind the brocade curtains, and I slowly walked to the podium, more or less ready to deliver my "Why I Should Be Your Senior Class President" speech. I held on to the podium like I had suction cups on my hands. My heart was setting a new world speed record.

My self-talk certainly wasn't helping. "What the heck am I doing here? Why would 800 students in 'da Bronx New York' listen to me? I'm a 17-year-old girl just out of the steel-girded cocoon of overprotective parents. Why am I doing this?"

I fully expected to be booed off the stage, ducking the (hopefully) empty milk cartons hurled at me. I had one eye on the exit as I started speaking. Then Holy s--t! Over 800 seniors were applauding and whistling their approval! I held tight to the podium and kept on with my still blurry vision for James Monroe High School's senior class.

This potent memory emerged one Saturday morning while digging through bins in my garage. As I sifted through faded photos and yellowed paper, it was clear when an opportunity to lead presented itself to me, even when it was the scariest thing to do, I take it.

When I entered the workforce, I served as a leader in several domains. My experiences include leading the largest reading program for underserved children in New York City, hundreds of staff, and then ushering technology into Wall Street major financial institutions. I then led global teams charged with large-scale initiatives.

In corporate America, I was one of a few women in the male-dominated worlds of finance and technology where women usually assumed clerical roles, not ones of leadership. The rich learning experiences of those years yielded my first book, *Cool Change: Turning Messy Emotions into Leadership Strengths,* where I shared stories of many fearless women who created a connection through a gift we all get but don't always use – our emotions.

Her Quote

"Emotion is not a four-letter word. While emotions can get messy, they offer the enormous service of helping us understand ourselves and others. And if we do make a mess, we're responsible for cleaning it up."
– Dr. Patricia (Pat) Baxter

"Uncle" Al was my dad's friend, mentor, and our hero as he gave Dad a job when he needed one. He lived with us for years and had a front-row seat to my teenage meltdowns and dumb decisions. "Patty – you're too emotional! THINK first!" he'd say. Interestingly, while he was no neuroscientist, Al had it right– it's about moving from the brain's reactive response center (the amygdala) and switching to the prefrontal cortex where "executive thinking" abilities reside. Though I knew little (correction – I knew nothing) about the "mechanics" of human emotion, I did know emotions unchecked could make things messy.

Decades later, the work of Harvard's Dr. Daniel Goleman and others that explored the power of emotional intelligence (referred to as EI) served as a compass for my doctoral research. In particular, I focused on EI's essential role of using emotions to manage workplace conflict.

Two questions intrigued me:

1. What are emotions? Why do they exist?

2. Do they matter anymore in the 21st-century workplace?

So, what are emotions? When I asked leaders through surveys and interviews, most would say emotion is happy, emotion is sad, etc., but that didn't answer the question – what **are** they? I read endless papers and articles searching for a way to explain emotion's qualities to the extent that a visitor from another galaxy would understand. Finally, I found one that fits perfectly:

"Emotions are short, intense, organized reactions to an event, person, or entity." (Izard, 1978)

While this definition works, it also scares me. When you realize you can have an emotional reaction to every single thing you encounter – people, objects, events, smells, sounds, etc. – it can be overwhelming. Studies indicate humans can experience 40,000 to 60,000 emotions in 24 hours, even as we sleep.

Why do we even have emotions?

Now that I know more about emotions, I recognize how they enrich our lives, serving us in three particular ways that govern how we think, behave, respond and serve others:

✦ Emotions help us examine our inner world and to understand ourselves and others in it.

+ Emotions help us manage relationships and assess how we interact with and understand one another. Whether you're in a difficult conversation or marketing your services, you must know how to interact in a way that helps you achieve your goal.

+ Emotions help us to act, do something, and make better decisions with all the data we receive through our senses.

Are women more "emotional" than men?

Accepted societal norms are hard to overcome. Women tend to be our designated caregivers while males are, to an extent, expected to act as providers. As I dug deeper, I found research that revealed this social construct isn't and needn't be a hard and fast rule. It shows gender differences exist in how and how often emotion is expressed; however, the results are far less consistent than expected based on popular convictions.

As a corporate-level coach to women, I observed that when the female leader did not demonstrate the appropriate or "right" level of emotion for the situation, she is vilified. (Of course, that level was arbitrary.) While emotions are a "standard issue" for all humans, when, how, and to whom they are shown can be a "darn if you do, darn if you don't" situation. Empathy, an EI attribute Harvard Business School and others view as critical to leadership success, is a trait women tend to demonstrate more openly. Oxytocin is released into the bloodstream as a hormone in response to love, and while in labor – it is the hormone that helps mothers and babies bond. This hormone may somehow contribute to why it may appear it's easier for women to show emotion and underscore a belief female leaders might be expected to show caregiving attributes more readily than males.

Advice for Her

Recognize you are not the emotion. We feel the emotion; however, you are not the emotion. Sadness and anger are emotions. Emotions come and go just like that. I cling to this quote from the Buddhist nun, Pema Chodron: "You are like the sky. Everything else is like the weather." Emotions come and go. They are to be observed, not judged.

You are totally responsible for your emotions and for managing them.

I encourage my coaching clients to reflect on how emotional resilience can help us know who we are, what triggers us, and to stay alert to the temptation to blame others for our feelings. I've had a later-in-life realization that no one can make you feel angry, ashamed, agitated, anxious, or afraid. Eleanor Roosevelt, who had her fair share of knockdown fights with emotion, said: "No one can make you feel inferior without your permission." Amen to that, sister.

Action Steps for Her

1. **Know yourself first.** Find a qualified professional to administer a certified EI assessment and review

those results with you. To select the best one for you, first understand what EI competencies are measured and how they can help your professional and personal growth. Develop a plan to improve *your* EI and review it regularly to stay conscious of areas to improve.

2. **Have a plan for regrouping when you've "lost it."** Everyone, I mean *everyone*, gets triggered to act out. Go for a walk and remind yourself everything you think and feel is temporary. If you're going to lose it, follow Mom's advice and count to 10. Why does it work? The neocortex will engage in a logical process and give you a few seconds to course correct.

3. **Do an emotional audit.** Say you've had a disagreement with a colleague. Even with a photographic (eidetic) memory, you may remember being cool and calm while your colleague says you went ballistic. This five-question emotional audit is a highly effective way to bring self-awareness and self-management to the forefront before conflict does any damage. Find a quiet place and consider/journal responses to these questions:

   1. What am I thinking?

   2. What am I feeling?

   3. What do I want now? What matters right now so I may achieve my goal?

   4. How am I getting in my way? What assumptions am I making that do not serve my objective?

5. What do I need to do ***differently*** now? What skills, tools, and insights from past experiences might help me move forward?

In an increasingly uncertain and divided world, remember we each can grow deeper connections through emotions. You are exceptionally well equipped to tap into and gifted with emotional intelligence that can inspire all of us on this "blue marble" and create health and wealth for all.

Live EI every day.

DR. PATRICIA (PAT) BAXTER

UNITED STATES

"Emotion is not a four-letter word" is Dr. Pat's mantra expressing her belief that emotion is most impactful as a *gift* we use to connect intelligently and positively to others, especially as emotions change the way we see the world and, as a result, how we view and treat one another.

A bilingual educator, executive consultant/coach and global team leader for Fortune 500 firms, Pat has served in many cultures and in industries including technology, customer service and financial services. Her doctorate is in Organizational Leadership and she has received the Emotional Intelligence Ambassador Award. Her books, *Cool Change: Turning Emotions into Leadership Strengths*© and *101 Ways to Grow an Awesome & Resilient Team Using Emotional Intelligence*© have received praise for their practical, real-world advice.

Website: www.patriciabaxter.com

LinkedIn: www.linkedin.com/in/patbaxter

Instagram: drpatbaxter

THE POWER OF
LEADERSHIP LOVE

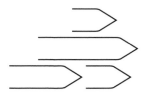

CHAPTER 15

CALLED TO LEAD - LOVE PRODUCTIVITY

DONNA HANSON, CSP

Before the internet and smartphones, workplace "productivity" was judged by when you arrived at work and the time you left. The longer the hours at the office, the more productive it was assumed you were.

With the evolution of technology, "productivity" defaulted to the number of emails sent to whom.

For 10 years, I experienced technology's impact in various administrative roles as it became ingrained in the everyday workplace. My passion for productivity, especially in leveraging computer software, ignited when I worked as a corporate trainer. In this role, I delivered full and half-day training in various software programs.

The training would typically encompass eight generic topics and a relaxing lunch at a nearby five-star hotel. Participants are expected to return to work "miraculously" transferring their new knowledge into workplace productivity.

The assumption was if they did not "get it" or remember everything, it was their fault!

I found this time challenging professionally. Classroom training covered topics deemed what attendees uniformly needed to know to be more productive at work. Simultaneously, participants were enthusiastic; most left training worried about catching up on the missed workday tasks, and unsure how to apply what they learned back to their work environment.

Disillusioned with the generic "one size fits all" classroom training results, I saw the need to explore how this could be improved.

Productivity is not something that happens. Productivity requires a sense of curiosity, an openness to development, and a recognition that working with technology can be improved. It requires lateral thinking and common knowledge sharing with colleagues to discover what you do not know.

For the last 20 years, I have worked with organizations to help them unlock productivity with standard technology, reducing business risk and stress, and improving the engagement and the development and wellbeing of their staff.

Becoming a productive leader with technology requires the courage to commit to rethinking how we use technology, how we engage and share information, and how this can make for a less stressed, more profitable, and productive workplace.

Her Quote

"You don't know what you don't know." – Donna Hanson

It is my favorite quote because it genuinely taps into technology's real intent and purpose.

I love how it creates "light bulb" moments for audiences. After a presentation, a group of women shared that they **thought** they were advanced but now realize they gained needed tools; I know my message resonates!

The technology was supposed to make it possible to achieve more, with increased productivity and less risk and stress. But instead, it has resulted in a "snowball effect" and repeatedly has people at the point of exhaustion. There is often an accepted underlying sense that being overloaded or always struggling with your workload is normal.

As a child born to post-depression era parents, my parents told me to work hard. The consensus was that putting in the long hours makes you a useful and valuable worker.

The concept of long hours equates to productivity still exists. Now productivity is measured by the number of emails sent, what time they are sent, and who is receiving the emails.

By merely saving yourself 15 minutes every workday, you will gain around 60 extra work hours a year. Think of what you could do with that spare time!

In the absence of courageous, innovative leaders to guide business practices with technology, workers endure long hours and unreasonable expectations such as being on-call via email.

Each next generation of technology promises to make our working lives more comfortable and deliver the "magic bullet" for productivity gains and profit increases. The expectation results in organizations and their people continuously needing to adapt. Often with little time to achieve the best outcomes before the "next big thing" is released and the cycle restarts.

"You don't know what you don't know" means challenging the way we work. Questioning what we do not know and how we can leverage technology to work smarter, reduce risk and stress, and increase workplace productivity.

"You don't know what you don't know" is not merely a quote; it should be a mantra to encourage you to be asking continually, could there be something that I do not know that could make me more productive?

Advice for Her

Being called to lead productively in business will not be easy, but it will be rewarding!

It means challenging the status quo and asking, "What might there be that I do not know?"

It means cultivating knowledge sharing with others.

It means being intentional with your time and managing your energy.

It means driving your priorities rather than being driven by the priorities of others.

You are called to lead; you likely already know **Why** you do what you do. What the highest priority is in your life. It may be family, contribution, or legacy. It does not matter what your **Why** is; what matters is that **YOU** know what your **Why** is.

Your **Why** is your driver toward leading productively.

It will keep you going instead of defaulting to old habits such as "we have always done it this way" or choosing to say yes when you know you should be saying no!

Productive leadership is being courageous enough to know with certainty what your focus is. You know when you feel yourself faltering, you can remind yourself of your **Why**.

You need to know you are worthy, that your time is valuable, and using it purposefully and productively means you are giving the best of yourself in every part of your life.

In time, productive leadership becomes a habit. Like exercise, it energizes you and is something that you reinforce daily. There will be times when you will not feel as productive as you want to be. At those times, it is essential to remind yourself of your **Why** and alter your actions to bring you back to leading productively.

Now it is time to step out on the metaphorical ledge.

To have faith in your abilities, and trust that if your intentions are good and start asking questions and taking action, you will be leading productively.

Know that you have got this. You have the capability and the capacity.

Know that you can do this, like a swimmer about to dive into the water at the Olympics, remind yourself that you know your stuff, and trust it is time to back yourself to dive in and succeed.

Now let us focus on taking action!

Action Steps for Her

Nothing happens without action.

Regardless of who you are, we only have 24 hours each day. Leading productively means budgeting your time as you would your money. You are asking yourself, "Is time lost on activities that add little value?"

You can reclaim time by asking these questions. I have provided some suggestions to help guide you.

1. What do you need to STOP doing?

- **STOP** multitasking – give yourself permission to focus on one thing at a time and do that thing well

- **STOP** saying yes to meetings that are unnecessary or that you need not attend

- **STOP** just accepting the way things are done, ask yourself, "Is there a better way?"

- **STOP** saying yes to everything; evaluate before you respond

- **STOP** leaving your email open all day; instead, read and respond in batches

2. What do you need to START doing?

- **START** by changing your email program, so it opens in your calendar, not your email, a reminder to help drive your day by your priorities

- **START** reducing your meeting length from one hour to 45 minutes

- **START** asking why have we always done it this way?

- **START** switching off entirely from work, for example, no reading email after 6 PM or block out times at weekends

- **START** sharing your knowledge and fostering curiosity. Learn from others

Leading productively starts with these two powerful questions and challenges the status quo.

Productive leadership requires courage to commit to change, often going back to simple, common-sense strategies.

For the moment, this is where our journey together ends.

It is now your turn to step up and apply these strategies to explore what you don't know and improve your productivity.

I hope what I have shared helps you personally and professionally and impacts the lives of those around you positively and profoundly.

I encourage you to revisit these strategies and journal your insights and learnings regularly. Know that I am behind you, beside you, and on your shoulder, cheering you on as you lead productively!

I would love to keep in touch, hear what you have done and help celebrate your achievements. Feel free to connect with me or reach out if I can help support you.

DONNA HANSON

CSP
AUSTRALIA

Australian Global Productivity Expert, Donna Hanson is a leader in business productivity with everyday technology. Her unique approach takes audiences on a journey that shifts their view of how they learn and use technology, and how they share knowledge in business.

With over 25 years' experience in delivering adult education and a degree in training and development, Donna *knows* what organizations really need to increase productivity, performance, and profits with everyday technology.

Donna has designed and delivered training programs for organizations such as Microsoft, IBM, BMW Group Australia and Village Roadshow along with many government departments. She is one of only a few people outside the U.S. accredited to deliver productivity training with Microsoft's own applications to Microsoft staff, and regularly appears in the Australian media.

Learn more

Website: www.donnahanson.com.au

LinkedIn: www.linkedin.com/in/donnahansoncsp

Twitter: @donna_hanson

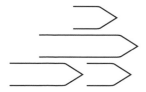

CHAPTER 16

CALLED TO LEAD – GIFTS OF PRESENCE

JESSICA DEVENISH

At the age of 15, I started working for my father's company after school. Recognized as the "boss's daughter" certainly gained me some friends (and some foes) right off the bat. At 18, I signed the largest client in the company, at that time. Finally, I earned my right to become a leader in my space. I was officially a respected sales executive! Earning this position provided the opportunity to build and train the sales team for a new location. A few years later, my father sold the company, and I longed for a new adventure. It was time to move on.

Or so I thought. My previous clients continuously reached out to me because expectations had fallen short since I had left. On a wing, a prayer, and the grace of my dad's mentorship, I started a new company doing what I did best – building relationships! During the day, I set out to build my clientele. In the evening, I completed the assigned work. As a newlywed, my husband was my greatest fan. Knowing our desire to become successful entrepreneurs we learned to lean on each other as business expanded. While he launched his business as a general contractor for residential homes, I handled payroll and accounting. We were all in – literally morning and night.

Ambition drove me to more opportunities. At 25, I partnered with my father to purchase a growing company in my industry that was staffed with 20 employees. I was excited to have a team to help me, as my morning and night routine needed some relief. Little did I know how hard it was going to be stepping into my new role. Ten years later, and I had to prove myself again. The team had been working together for several years and had no idea who I was, what my credentials were, or if they should trust me. History repeated itself. My now title of "owner" certainly gained me some quick friends and some quicker foes; the manager being one of them. He did not make it easy for me. With my years of grit, I was up for the challenge.

It was August 1997 and my husband and I welcomed our first-born child; she was less than a week old when the purchase of my new company was final. With two new companies and one new baby, I became a mom and entrepreneur concurrently growing my family and my businesses. Twenty years and five kids later, our kids are grown, and business is joyful. Two ambitious young adults, on the road to launching what has now come to be known as the Devenish Duo.

Executive leaders accept many responsibilities to ensure the success of the company and a profitable bottom line. Operational processes ensure consistency, accuracy, and client satisfaction. Workflows set teams up for success with a blueprint that offers clear expectations, roles and smooth operations. Company culture stabilizes a collaborative and productive environment.

With these tools and processes in place, one could believe they have all they need to achieve success. However, a genuinely great leader recognizes that the most important part of the business is *our people*. They are the faces of our business, and in time become our business family. No matter the type of business we own, manage, or to which industry we belong, we are all in the *People Business*. Words echoed by my father's mentorship.

It is our role to set budgets and develop processes to quantify and qualify efficiencies, key performance indicators and future growth. When it comes to human beings, there is no way to quantify the capacity of potential inside each of us. Our potential is infinite, and it is for this reason that the greatest responsibility leaders have is to prioritize their employees as number one! First, it is critical to create a culture where the team is built on gratitude, creativity, and communication. Culture sets the tone, and when done correctly will guide the team to achieve their infinite potential. Individually and collectively.

Her Quote

"Our potential is infinite when we unleash our creative power with a grateful heart." – Jessica Devenish

Advice for Her

If someone were to ask me how to build such a team with a collaborative culture, I would share three secret gifts I've learned over the years:

1. Gift of Gratitude
2. Gift of Creativity
3. Gift of Communication

The Gift of Gratitude is the gateway to abundance. If we are focusing on wanting more, then when do we express and live in gratitude? There are two realities always seeking our attention: one is lack and the other is abundance. Gratitude elevates our heart space and creates a magnetic force that pulls in greatness to us. Where our focus goes, it grows.

One of the great writers of our time, Earl Nightingale, teaches that "We become what we think about."

When we think grateful thoughts, we feel grateful, resulting in finding more opportunities to share gratitude. As a leader, when we lean into *knowing* that gratitude is a magnet for greatness, we tap into a high vibrational feeling of abundance.

The Gift of Creativity inspires innovative thought, production, and solutions. When we step aside the rigid walls of a guided process, creativity flows in a higher level capacity. For instance, if you give your team an opportunity to fulfill a customer's needs, you give them the creative energy that comes from within their being. They are affirmed that their voice and ideas matter. They recognize their own value to the company and authentically work harder.

The Gift of Communication is of the utmost importance in connecting leaders and their team members in an open and honest way. Words carry power, and each word you speak matters. Words draw or bring energy in or suck energy out.

There are four engaging aspects of how words are experienced:

1. Words we speak

2. Words we hear

3. Words we read

4. Words we write

Speaking. Are the words that you speak positive and expressing affirmation, grace, and kindness? Do you express gratitude to team members both daily and when most appropriate? Express gratitude with a compassionate "thank you" and you contagiously light a flame to inspire shared enthusiasm with others. Spoken words can very well be your voice to the world and your environment. So, what are you saying?

Hearing. On a daily basis, what are you listening to? Do you choose content such as podcasts or audiobooks that are uplifting and inspiring you to be a "leader's leader?" How are you engaging in the LOVE OF LIFE and gratitude? Music is a language too, have you considered having a music service in your business environment?

Reading. Do the books you read lift your vibration? I believe the people that we meet and the books that we read can mold and shape our character. What are you reading? Have you read a book with your team?

Writing. Do you journal? When putting thoughts to paper there is often a beautiful transfer of emotions from your head space to your heart space. When you are *seeing* the emotion written in front of you it can *heighten your vibration* in a new way. Reflect and write down how you are feeling. Feelings are emotions. Emotions are energy in motion.

Action Steps for Her

1. **Cultivate the Gift of Gratitude.** Embark on a *gratitude* journey. Start and end each day noting your grateful moments. Start with a simple person, place and thing. Outgoing vibrations of gratitude increase and magnify more abundance. By being in a grateful place, you enter a higher vibration, and in this state of being you invite more goodness to flow into your life and the lives of people surrounding you.

2. **Cultivate the Gift of Creativity.** Embark on a *think tank* journey. Invite a variety of staff members to a meeting with a specific process in mind that needs some fine-tuning and improvement. To begin the meeting, ask each person to write their "title" on a piece of paper and fold it up. Next, present the operational process that needs attention. Set the stage for a safe environment where no idea is a bad idea. Before everyone begins sharing, have them crumple up their title and throw it in the trash! This establishes a level playing field and creates common ground to share and collaborate. Watch the creativity *flow* with abundance.

3. **Cultivate the Gift of Communication.** Embark on a *survey* journey. Invite your team to give feedback through an anonymous survey. You choose the questions. They openly communicate their answers. Invite their *words* to guide you to greatness.

Communication is a demonstration of one's energy. You are constantly sending out a force-field of energy in the form of vibrations all around you. Your vibrations are real and have the ability to power a team just as electricity powers your place of business.

Plug in and prepare to lead… Ready, Set, Gift!

JESSICA DEVENISH

UNITED STATES

Jessica Devenish, Co-Founder of Devenish Duo, is a serial entrepreneur, keynote speaker, executive coach, and transformation guide. She specializes in working with high-impact executives to find their joy and live a life of inner standing and abundance.

Connection is the heartbeat of our experiences. Jessica integrates her experiential wisdom, mindfulness practices and emotional intelligence knowledge to lead clients to achieve their absolute full potential.

Jessica healed herself of a recurrent pituitary brain tumor through the power of emotional healing and energy work. She has personally and professionally navigated through entrepreneurship, success, challenges, failures, grief, loss, betrayal, trauma, and parenting a child with mental illness and suicidal ideation.

Her work enriches lives. People thrive through the power of connection, love, and an abundant mentality, and with Jessica, you will achieve the fulfilling life you desire.

Learn more

Website: www.devenishduo.com

LinkedIn: www.linkedin.com/in/jessicadevenish

Facebook: www.facebook.com/devenishduo

ABBONDANZA!!!

Barbara Baron

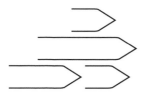

CHAPTER 17

CALLED TO LEAD – ABBONDANZA: FOOD. FAMILY. FAITH

BARBARA BARON, MS, RDN, CDN, FAND

Growing up in an Italian American Catholic family, I was surrounded by strong faith, embraced with love, and supplied with an abundance of good food – ABBONDANZA! There wasn't ever any skimping! Fresh fruit and vegetables, bread, meats and dairy were all purchased at small specialty food stores. My mom's version of "fast food" was spaghetti aglio e olio (garlic and oil), usually with zucchini or leftover broccoli and topped with grated cheese. Instilled in us by our grandparents, a meal on the table symbolized the path to health and wealth.

Even in today's fast-paced culture, meals remain the center of many family gatherings, and in my family, we helped with the preparation and cooking as soon as we could walk, an inescapable task. Ever since I was five, I remember cleaning green beans and washing fresh escarole for salad. What felt like a mundane chore at the time, I now recognize as one of the greatest gifts I received. It's the gift that keeps on giving. Ask my kids!

It was in the kitchen, not the boardroom, where I learned confidence and life skills. Growing up in a family of five, I mastered patience as I waited for everyone to be seated at the table before we picked up a fork. My ears became attuned to the art of listening as my parents and grandparents shared stories of their childhood. It was beyond what any history book could teach.

Studies prove that meals nourish us more than our bodies. Children who eat together with their family have healthier weights, better nutrition, better grades, lower risk of smoking and drug use, and parents have a better relationship with their teens. The gift of ABBONDANZA! is much more than studies alone can quantify. It is a feeling of satisfaction and joy from food, love of family, and intense spirituality, which all significantly contribute to confidence, physical wellbeing, and emotional wellness, all preparing us to live richly at home and thrive richly in business.

As a registered dietitian nutritionist of 35 years, I have seen all types of diets, and one fundamental lesson that I learned is when we do not intertwine nourishment with our body, minds, and hearts, we live a life that is unfulfilled, yearning for more. Instead of yearning for more, embrace the spirit of ABBONDANZA! It is the feeling of having plenty. The experience satisfies more than just physical hunger and nutrition. It satisfies your appetite to connect, to feel important, to be heard, to share your day, to dream and to be loved.

For me, Christmas Eve dinner is the epitome of ABBONDANZA! At five, it was my responsibility to set the table. At 16, I graduated and learned how to prepare the lobster for a traditional Italian Christmas Eve dinner of seven fish with my mother and grandmother right by my side. Three generations united. Now that I am a grown woman, I am responsible for buying the ingredients; I quickly learned that lobsters are expensive! I wonder how, each year, my mom afforded to feed a family of 20 relatives, sometimes even a last-minute guest. There was always room for one more at the table.

My family was not wealthy; Dad was a small businessman, a machinist, Mom was a clerk, my grandfather worked on deck corking cargo ships, and my grandmother was a seamstress. Yet, by God's grace, year after year, our plates were full of seven types of fish, including the most expensive menu item, lobster. The family pulled together to keep the tradition alive while reminding me of the "miracle of feeding the multitude," the story in the Bible when Jesus easily fed a crowd of 5,000 with five loaves of bread and two fish. There was always plenty for everyone, and after breaking bread together, they were all satisfied. ABBONDANZA!

Her Quote

"ABBONDANZA! Break bread with family and friends together around the table. You will nourish your mind, body, and soul with confidence and compassion!" – Barbara Baron

When it comes to preparing the meal, I have witnessed the love and commitment among family and friends sharing traditions, culinary hacks, and how to choose and prepare healthy food.

Have you ever heard this ancient Chinese proverb? "Give a man a fish, and you feed him for a day. Teach a man to fish, and you feed him for a lifetime." ABBONDANZA!

Advice for Her

According to a Harris Poll, 87% of Americans sit down to dinner at least once a week, while 5% never have family dinners. Through the years, I have experienced such vast variations in how today's families break bread together; it hurts my heart that our culture is dismissing the essential life-giving, family-loving and soul-enriching practice that has been the centrifugal force of the family connection for centuries. I have made it my personal mission, in my professional practice and personal life, to encourage efforts to share more meals together at the table, sharing that feeling of abundance. Consider the following lessons to nestle into that pocket in your life where you feel fully and richly nourished.

✦ Operate from a place of hope, not fear, or lack

My grandparents and parents were role models living from a mindset of abundance, especially their faith. Keep an open heart to receive the blessings from prayers by family and friends, as they become our spiritual food that paves the way to clarity for health, wealth, and prosperity.

✦ Dish up a new experience around family meals

It is never too late. Adopt the spirit of ABBONDANZA! as a goal for your family to experience and build it from there. When healthy meals are a fun activity and loving experience, our cups runneth over with love, memories, confidence, compassion, and memories.

✦ Celebrate, not dissipate, each unique family treasure from your ancestors

Connect or reconnect with your grandparents, great aunts, and great uncles to learn more about your heritage and how to make traditional dishes. Bring richness to your life.

✦ Share gratitude by setting loving intentions at mealtimes

Choose calm over chaos when cooking and eating, despite challenges with hectic schedules. Create joyful conversations over good-tasting healthy food. As you set a sauce to simmer on the stove, remind yourself that you are crafting a deep, rich, flavorful meal made with love.

✦ Build a healthier you one meal at a time®

Open the door to better health and opportunities with those you love to prosper and nourish your own mind, body, and soul. ABBONDANZA!

Action Steps for Her

Four simple steps to elevate confidence, conversation, and compassion during every meal for each person around the table.

1. **Take Charge.** Take out the calendar and start small. Find at least one time during the week when everyone is available for a family meal. The hour doesn't matter as much as making this time with your family a priority. Pledge that same day and time of the week to establish a habit. The more often you plan and write it on your calendar, the greater success.

2. **Be Creative.** Family meals don't always have to be around a table, they don't always have to be prepared at home, nor does it have to be dinner. Plan a picnic or post-game meal or snack. Don't worry if you don't have time to cook. Many supermarkets now offer healthy ready-to-eat foods or have foods already prepared. Sometimes keeping it super simple is better. A bowl of vegetable soup, a sandwich and glass of milk make a quick, easy, balanced, and nutritious meal. Buon appetito! Finally, if the dinner hour is too hectic, consider a family breakfast or lunch. Whatever works – your rules, your way!

3. **Share Compassion and Conversation.** A whitepaper by the Hartman Group Food Marketing Institute Foundation reports more than one-third of family dinners are missed due to adults who live alone. Invite a relative or friend to join your meal-time fun. Sharing dinner with grandparents is an opportunity to learn about your family history and creates an appreciation of different mealtime traditions or cultures.

4. **Build Quality Time, Kitchen Sense and Confidence.** Get your children and teens involved! They can help set the table, clean, cut, chop, stir, follow recipes, and even clean up. Practicing all these "jobs" increases reading, math, planning, positioning, organizing, confidence, responsibility, joy, laughter and fun. Plus, manners at the table are always impressive: "Please." "Thank you." "Wait your turn." Time spent in the kitchen is never a waste because at some point they will move out, go to college, become employed, and maybe have their own family to teach. Remember, "When you teach a man to fish, it lasts a lifetime." Surround them with family, food, faith, fun, and skills, and they will always live with the spirit of ABBONDANZA!

BARBARA BARON

MS, RDN, CDN, FAND
UNITED STATES

Barbara Baron is a Registered Dietitian Nutritionist, Fellow of the Academy of Nutrition and Dietetics, and the Founder/CEO of Barbara Baron Nutrition.

With 30-plus years of professional experience in food and nutrition, and having raised two active boys, Barbara understands the challenges people face in preparing healthy meals.

As an enthusiastic and engaging professional speaker and Family Meals Dietitian®, Barbara brings the feeling of ABBONDANZA! sharing nutritious meal ideas, culinary hacks, and mindful eating tips to businesses, associations, and families who want more time, energy, and better health. Her audiences learn how to integrate better nutrition, easy planning, quicker preparation, and enjoy more meals around the table with family and friends. Barbara speaks to organizations such as Mentoring in Medicine, a sponsored program of the National Medical Association.

Learn more

Website: www.barbarabaron.com

LinkedIn: www.linkedin.com/in/barbarabaronrdn

Instagram: barbara.baron

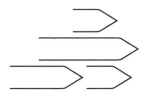

CHAPTER 18

CALLED TO LEAD - LIFE BY DESIGN, NOT DEFAULT:

A PROVEN FRAMEWORK FOR CREATING A LIFE YOU LOVE

SYDNE JACQUES, PE, CSP

As a civil engineer, I worked hard to earn my degree, then studied intensely for months to pass two challenging full-day exams that engineers must take four years apart to earn a professional engineering license. That status gives me the knowledge and authority to design and build things like roads, bridges, and buildings. I didn't know that the most important thing I would learn to design and build was not infrastructure for my community but to design and build a life I love. Creating a life by design, not default, has given me joy, the opportunity to make memories with my family and serve my community in more ways than I ever thought possible.

I have worked in my industry for many years, and I love working with people. I realized that being a people-person was rare in engineering and that my life, and my approach to life, was different. I knew I had a calling to lead to share my model. Creating a life by design has its ups and downs, and I've had plenty of those along the way. But because I always had a vision of where I was going and what I wanted my life to be, it has been a fantastic ride and more incredible than I could have hoped.

Her Quote

"I am TOUGH, I am SMART, I am STRONG, I can do this… GRRRRRR." – Sydne Jacques

When I was a freshman in college, there was only one other female studying engineering. Her name was Cathy, and we became best friends (and as women do, we are still in touch 40 years later). Engineering classes were challenging for both of us. We were smart enough, but the formulas, equations, and problem solving seemed to come so much easier to most of the guys in our classes.

One Friday night, Cathy and I were in the library studying for a big test that we would take the following Tuesday. At 10:00 PM, the security guard came in and kicked us out of the library because it was closing. We packed our heavy backpacks full of books and headed over to the physics building and studied two more hours until a different security guard kicked us out at midnight. As we were walking home from the physics building, we asked ourselves, "Are we crazy? Why are we doing this? It's SO hard! Do we want to be engineers when we grow up?" As we were walking and talking, we decided the answer to these questions was YES! Yes, we are crazy, and yes, we do want to be engineers when we grow up.

The next few moments will forever live in my memory; Cathy and I came up with our "team" motto walking across campus that night, and we still say it to each other, our kids, and the women we mentor today. We pinky-promised to be there for each other no matter how hard it was, and we promised to say this mantra every single day, "I am TOUGH, I am SMART, I am STRONG, I can do this… GRRRRRR." Making the "GRRRRR" tiger sound loud and proud from your chest brings amazing power. Try it!

By following this framework and reminding myself every day that, "I am TOUGH, I am SMART, I am STRONG, I can do this… GRRRRRR," I have been able to create a business that generates over $1 million a year while I continue to work from home (unless I am getting paid to travel and speak for clients all over the world.) I have done this while raising four amazing kids who are now adults, working to maintain a happy marriage, serving in my church and community, and even winning a gold medal playing basketball in the Senior Olympics!

Find an accountability buddy (studies prove we are 90% more likely to accomplish our goals when we have an accountability partner). It's worth it, I promise!

Advice for Her

To start creating a life by design, I had to think about what I knew for sure. What is in my bones?

By the time I graduated college, I knew for sure:

1. I wanted to be a mom. My ideal picture included four children (I like even numbers, and with this number, everyone has a riding buddy when you go to Disneyland).

2. I wanted to have my own business. When I was in college, I had *no* idea what that would be, and for a long time, I thought maybe I would create a side-gig in addition to my regular job.

3. I always wanted to stay active and healthy.

4. I wanted to be able to live a life where I put relationships first. I didn't want my relationships with God, my family, or my friends to ever be at risk because of my career.

The incredible thing about designing your life is that each of us gets to do it differently, just the way we want it. By asking ourselves what do we know for sure and what do we want out of life? I am so excited to share my successful model, I have taught this to thousands of people, and it has proven successful time after time.

Action Steps for Her

This model is the same model I would use to design and build a road, a bridge, or a campground, and it works like a charm for also creating lives!

1. **Vision.** Taking the time to create an image and a plan for your future is a critical investment. When I first started my business, part of my vision was to earn $10,000/month working from home. It took me a few years to accomplish, but my goal was clear, and I was determined. I wasn't the least bit surprised when I achieved it. Ask yourself, "What do I want to accomplish with my health (both physical and mental), my finances, my relationships, my spirituality, and my personal growth?" This first challenge begins with a commitment to take the time to get away, even for a couple of hours. Go in nature if possible, and don't take a phone. Take a notebook and a pen and get to work!

2. **Data.** As an engineer, I have learned we can't make the right decisions without data. This second challenge is to collect data for each vision area. To gather data, ask questions like, "How much money am I currently making? How many calories am I currently consuming? How much time do I spend one-on-one with those I love in an average week?" There are

several ways to collect data on your happiness, such as "On a scale of 1-10, how happy are you today?" It is essential to establish benchmarks to be able to measure progress.

3. **Design.** This is a favorite step of mine and where this process gets fun! Once you have a vision and gathered data, the next step is to create a design for the different areas of your life. It is essential to define the "gaps" between where you are and where you want to be and then have fun creating your individual, specific, and intentional design. For example, every year, I create a new business plan of what I want to accomplish for my financial design. Every year, I create a design of my exercise and fitness goals, and for the last three years I have increased my muscle mass and decreased my body fat (not bad for an old lady in her late 50s). These goals are accomplished by applying "design" to all the crucial areas of my life to create one amazing life.

4. **Construction.** I love being at a construction site. It is so energizing to see the enormous pieces of equipment moving dirt, digging holes, getting things done. But companies would never dream of sending their bulldozers and track hoes out to the project without a design. Once the design step is complete, it is time to get to work and begin construction. These lessons are the same when it comes to constructing your life. It will never go as planned, but you will continually make progress.

5. **Celebrations!** When I work on big construction projects, and we get close to the end, I notice that most of the engineers and contractors get antsy to move on and start focusing on the next project. I put my foot down and call time out. I insist that before we move on to the next project, we need to acknowledge then celebrate the excellent work we have accomplished. One of my rules for life is that you should always have something to look forward to! Maybe it's a vacation, getting a pedicure, a girl's getaway, or a bubble bath. It doesn't have to be expensive, but it does have to be a celebration for YOU and what YOU have accomplished!

SYDNE JACQUES

PE, CSP
UNITED STATES

Sydne Jacques is a civil engineer, speaker and is the "the engineer with a personality." She built a 26-year-old, award-winning consulting company with clients around the world. Through her learning models she trained over 12,000 individuals in Leadership, Communication and Trust. She is passionate about mentoring women!

Named as one of "30 Women to Watch" by *Utah Business Magazine* and her company, Jacques & Associates, was rated the 12th top women-owned business in Utah. Sydne serves on the board of directors for the Associated General Contractors of Utah, the National Advisory Board for the College of Engineering at Brigham Young University and Working Moms Connection.

This farm girl from Montana is happily married, a mother of four and even earned a gold medal in the Huntsman Senior Games for Women's Basketball.

Learn more

Website: www.sydnespeaks.com

LinkedIn: www.linkedin.com/in/sydne-jacques/

Twitter: @gosydne

YOUR POWER TO LEAD

You are called to lead. Take what you need now, leave the rest for the future. This is a guide book. Please keep it close, and when you need advice or tips from a mentor, pick it up and reread it.

The authors all journal; writing helps us understand where we are and where we are going. Throughout this book, there are points where you stopped and pondered. Take that as a cue to write and discover yourself.

This book is yours to grow by, feel connected, and know that you are not alone. Within this book are women who have been there and done that and have gained wisdom through their process.

You have our contact information, and we want to hear from you. Write to us, become part of our communities, invite us to speak at your conferences, or be on a panel. Follow us on social media. We are here for you today and will be here in 10 years.

The world needs your leadership savviness. We want you to thrive. May our paths cross soon.

Remember to be bold, brave, seen, heard, and paid well.

Enjoy your journey,

Pegine

Power Women Worldwide

NOTES

_____

_____

_____

_____

_____

_____

_____

_____

_____

_____

_____

_____

_____

_____

_____

_____

_____

_____

_____

_____

_____

_____

_____

_____

_____

_____

_____

_____

_____